# CONCILIUM
*Religion in the Seventies*

# CONCILIUM

*Religion in the Seventies*

Volume 76: Church and World

# NEW QUESTIONS
# ON GOD

Edited by
Johannes B. Metz

Herder and Herder

1972
HERDER AND HERDER NEW YORK
232 Madison Avenue, New York 10016

# CONTENTS

# PART I
ARTICLES

Johannes B. Metz

# The Future in the
# Memory of Suffering

## I

CONFIDENCE in the supposed gradual evolution of technological civilization has gone. If "progress" exists at all, it is only in opposition to its naïve generalization (as in some crude futurologies). Increasingly, the warm stream of teleology that helped our way of thinking in the past is drying up. Teleological reliance on a growing reconciliation of man with nature has collapsed; with its disappearance we notice for the first time how profoundly and tenaciously it gripped us, conditioning even our philosophical and theological interpretations of the future. But now Sisyphus suddenly reappears next to Prometheus, Camus next to Teilhard, Monod next to Whitehead. . . .[1]

We are becoming ever more conscious of the dangers and antagonisms that arise when technological and economic processes are left to their "natural" suasions and our political and social control systems break down: dying cities, ruined environmental systems, population explosions, chaotic information channels, an increasingly aggressive and vicious intensification of the North-South conflict, leading possibly to a new outcome of the East-West power struggle, and so on. In addition there is the threat posed to man's apparent identity and freedom by the growing possibilities of psychological and genetic manipulation. One also

[1] The present text is based on a paper given at a theological congress in New York in October 1971, involving debate and dialogue with "process theologians" and Teilhardists. Some passages arise from that confrontation.

9

suspects that, left to itself, the technologico-economic planning of man's future will produce the wholly adapted human being whose dreams and imagination can no longer keep up and are suppressed by the functionalism of technical systems; whose freedom degenerates into an instinctive animal adaptability to the superior power and complexity of preformed behaviour patterns; and who has been deprived of the world as something over against him, in order, in fact, to rob him of the need any longer to experience it personally. The purely technologically and economically planned production of man's future would seem to foreshadow the very disappearance of man as the being who has nourished himself on the historical substance of his freedom: on, that is, the power to find an alternative despite all need to conform. Hence there is no lack today of voices to follow up Nietzsche's proclamation of the "death of God" with that of the "death of man": the paralysis of human spontaneity and the burial of man in the grave of an economico-technical structuralism; and the fear that human thinking is losing its dialectical tension with the *status quo* and is being integrated with an all-encroaching and anonymous production process.

This situation seems to me to forbid any discussion of the future in non-subjective categories: development, progress or even "process". Instead we have to ask: whose development, whose progress, and whose process? And: development, progress and process in what direction? The question of the future of our technological civilization is a question not primarily of technology, but of the control and application of technology and economico-technological processes; a problem not primarily of means but of ends, and of the establishment of priorities and preferences. This means, however, that it is primarily a political and fundamentally a social problem.

But how can politics become the primary *topos* in our technological society for investigation of the future? Isn't politics, as something self-sufficient, set over against technology and economics in its death throes? Isn't there a growing anonymous dictatorship of structures and processes compared with which the dictatorship of individuals and parties seems harmless? Kenneth Boulding writes: "We can conceive of a world where an invisible dictatorship is still making use of democratic forms of government." Isn't the euthanasia of politics coming closer in our technological society? Aren't we witnessing an increasing self-paralysis of political reason and its consequent degeneration into instrumental reason in the service of technological and economic processes and their anonymous "power-systems"? Where are we to find a politics capable of controlling these systems and extricating them from the contradictions and catastrophes apparent today?

Would something like a radical "scientification" of politics help here? Certainly political life is becoming increasingly less capable of doing without the mediation and mobilization of scientific knowledge. Yet it is not science which constitutes and guarantees the authenticity of political consciousness as opposed to technological controls. Our modern sciences themselves are technological essentially and not merely incidentally; this is, in fact, a presupposition for their success and is grounded in the mode of cognition specific to them as sciences. Admittedly this raises a multitude of questions that cannot be pursued here. I would remark only that if a politics is to be more than a successful accommodation to the control systems of technical and economic processes, it must be grounded in something more and something other than science (as we know and understand it today).

Obviously this kind of politics will exist only when there is a fundamental change in our political life. But not the conversion of politics into purely technological administration and a computer-politics which in its programming merely reproduces the above-mentioned dilemmas, not an old-style decision-politics, and not Machiavellianism, a kind of stone-age politics in the twentieth century. What we need in the long run is a new form of political life and new political structures. Only when that arrives will there be any humane cultures at all in the future. In this sense, "politics" is actually the new name for culture (and in this sense, too, any theology which tries to reflect on Christian traditions in the context of world problems is also a "political theology"). I shall now mention some aspects of this new orientation and structural pattern of political awareness.

Our situation demands a new association between politics and morals, one which refuses to remain content with the kind of trivial affluent-society morality which we retain in the liberal distinction between politics and morals. As Jürgen Habermas says: "There are indications that developed social systems already accept, or are on the point of accepting, certain international imperatives of life—namely, the elimination of war as a legitimate means of settling conflicts, and the removal of mass poverty and disparities in economic development. Even where these systems do not at present offer adequate motives for the solution of such global problems, one thing is nevertheless already clear: a solution of these problems is hardly possible without the application throughout life of those universalist norms which were hitherto required only in the private sphere. Someone still tied to the old categories might call this the 'moralization' of politics. But this kind of idea ought not to be dismissed—simply on those grounds —as naïve enthusiasm."

This connection between politics and morals cannot be ordained from above, and can and should not be allowed to relapse into the political canonization of a particular moral system. It requires the mobilization of spiritual and moral forces by means of a radical democratization of the social infrastructure, a nourishing from below of freedom and effective responsibility.

The form of political life that would allow a culture of freedom in our economico-technological processes cannot, in my opinion, afford to ignore the reserves of moral and political imagination that appear in the present subcultures and counter-cultures of our technological society. Far more than the conventional generation conflict is expressed in this "youth culture". It is, in a certain sense, our Western form of the Cultural Revolution, the experimental quest for an alternative to the control systems of our technological society. Anyone who merely expects the escapists to return penitently like lost sheep to the established system has misunderstood both this culture and his own situation.

Of course this new political life, whose aims are not confined to what is deemed plausible by our economico-technological controls, does not intend to bypass technology and economics altogether. There is neither an alternative to technology, nor (to date) an alternative technology. What is sought for and demanded is instead a new form of mediation, a new instrumental control of this technology and these technical and economic processes. One thing, above all, must be avoided: the dissolution of political imagination and political action into the pure business of planning. Only the independence of the political dimension can guarantee the possibility of a humane future.

You will perhaps remember the story of the fight between the two giants. One of them is weaker and is on the brink of defeat yet manages to keep going and finally free himself from the other's grasp. He is able to do this because a tiny hunchback sits in his ear, urging him on and continually whispering new defensive ploys. This might serve as a parable for the struggle between technology and politics, between purely economico-technological planning and a political draft for the future. Political imagination will prevent itself from ultimate absorption by the restrictive grasp of technology, so long as it keeps the moral imagination and power to resist that have grown out of the memory of the suffering accumulated in history. The dwarf stands for the memory of this suffering: in our advanced social systems, suffering is pictured as insignificant, ugly and better kept out of sight.

Political consciousness *ex memoria passionis*, political action in the memory of mankind's history of suffering: this could indicate an understanding of politics that would lead to new possibilities and new criteria for the mastering of technological and economic processes. It offers inspiration for a new form of solidarity, of responsibility towards those most distant from us, inasmuch as the history of suffering unites all men like a "second nature". It prevents a purely technical understanding of freedom and peace; it excludes any form of freedom and peace at the expense of the suppressed history of suffering of other nations and groups. It forces us to look at the public *theatrum mundi* not merely from the standpoint of the successful and the established, but from that of the conquered and the victims. This recalls the function of the court fool in the past: he represented an alternative (rejected, vanquished or oppressed) to his master's policy; his function was strictly political and in no way "purely aesthetic". His politics was, so to speak, a politics of the memory of suffering—as against the traditional political principle of "woe to the conquered", and against the Machiavellian ruler. Today it is a question of sublating the "division of labour" in political life between the powerful on the one hand, and the "fool" with his powerless imagination of suffering on the other. Here I see the significance of a new association of politics and morals. From it there ultimately emerges a conception of political life and political responsibility for which the great moral and religious traditions of mankind could also, possibly, be mobilized, once they have been comprehended at their deepest level of meaning.

## II

Christianity does not introduce God subsequently as a kind of "stop-gap" into this conflict about the future; instead, it tries to keep alive the memory of the crucified Lord, this specific *memoria passionis*, as a dangerous memory of freedom in the social systems of our technological civilization. This assertion needs more detailed development and explication. I shall now mention some of the most important aspects.

1. First of all, a category that I have already used quite often in the course of these reflections on the theme of the "future" requires more exact delineation: this is the category of "memory". What prevents memory from being a traditionalistic, even a reactionary category when it is used as so fundamental a characterization of the future? How is it not a bourgeois counter-conception to hope, one leading us treacherously away from the risks of our future? In what sense can memory function as a practical and critical, and even dangerously emancipatory, force?

There are some very different kinds of memories. There are those in which we just do not take the past seriously enough: memories in which the past becomes a paradise without danger, a refuge from our present disappointments—the memory of the "good old days". There are memories which bathe everything from the past in a soft, conciliatory light. "Memory transfigures", we say, and at times we experience this in a rather drastic form, for example when old soldiers exchange war yarns at a regimental dinner. War as an inferno is obliterated from such memories: what seems to remain is only the adventure experienced long ago. Here the past is filtered through a harmless cliché: everything dangerous, oppressive and demanding has vanished from it: it seems deprived of all future. In this way, memory can easily become a "false consciousness" of our past and an opiate for our present.

But there is another form of memory: there are dangerous memories, memories which make demands on us. There are memories in which earlier experiences break through to the centre-point of our lives and reveal new and dangerous insights for the present. They illuminate for a few moments and with a harsh steady light the questionable nature of things we have apparently come to terms with, and show up the banality of our supposed "realism". They break through the canon of all that is taken as self-evident, and unmask as deception the certainty of those "whose hour is always there" (Jn. 7. 6). They seem to subvert our structures of plausibility. Such memories are like dangerous and incalculable visitants from the past. They are memories we have to take into account; memories, as it were, with future content. "Remembrance of the past", says a contemporary philosopher, "can allow dangerous insights to emerge, and society as it is established would seem to fear the subversive contents of this memory." It is not by chance that the destruction of memory is a typical measure of totalitarian rule. The enslavement of men begins when their memories of the past are taken away. All forms of colonialization are based on this principle. Every rebellion against suffering is fed by the subversive power of remembered suffering. In this sense, suffering is in no way a purely passive, inactive "virtue". It is, or can be, the source of socially emancipatory action. And in this sense the memory of accumulated suffering continues to resist the cynics of modern political power.

There is an obvious danger today that everything in our consciousness that is determined by memory, everything outside the calculations of our technico-pragmatic reason, will be equated with superstition and left to the private whim of the individual. But this doesn't necessarily mean that we are freer and more "enlightened". We merely fall prey to the dominant illusions all the more easily and are deceived in another way. There are many examples. In this sense the remembrance of accumulated suffering contradicts the contemporary prophets of the disappearance of history. This memory prevents us from understanding history either as a mere background for an occasional festive interpretation of our existence, or merely as distanced material for historical criticism. As the remembered history of suffering, history retains the form of "dangerous tradition". This subversive tradition resists any attempt to sublate and still it by means of a purely affirmative attitude to the past (as, for example, in hermeneutical theories) and by means of a wholly critical attitude to the past (as, for instance, in ideology criticism). The "mediation" of the memory of suffering is always practical.

2. We must confront the fact that this memory is a memory of *suffering: memoria passionis*. In our social life there is a kind of taboo preventing or impairing insight into the essentially cognitive and practical function of suffering.

Modern scientific knowledge is marked by the model of a dominative knowledge of nature, and in this view man understands himself anthropologically above all as the dominative subject in relation to nature. *Scientia et potentia in idem coincidunt*: Bacon's proposition characterizes the modern conception of science as dominative knowledge. Accordingly, in a society universally determined by this kind of scientific knowledge, other forms of human behaviour and knowledge (such as suffering, pain, mourning, but also joy, play, and so on) enjoy only a functional and derived validity, and are largely underestimated in a cognitive and critical sense. Hence it is significant that there should be a kind of *anti-knowledge ex memoria passionis* forming in our society, in which the existing identification of "praxis" with "domination of nature" is banished.

Our idea of history is also unilaterally affected by a screening out of the importance of suffering. We tend, consciously or unconsciously, to define history as the history of what has prevailed, as the history of the successful and the established: in historical studies, too, a kind of Darwinism in the sense of the principle of selection (*"Vae victis!"*) tends to prevail. Again it is of decisive importance that a kind of *anti-history* should develop out of the memory of suffering—an understanding of history in which the vanquished and destroyed alternatives would also be taken into account: an understanding of history *ex memoria passionis* as a history of the vanquished.

It also seems to me important to stress the *anti-teleological* and *anti-ontological* character of suffering—not least of all as against certain tendencies within theology itself. I should like to expand this point briefly.[2] There is a teleological and finalistic mediation between nature and man. This would seem to be confirmed by modern natural science, wherever, as in biology, it becomes anthropology. One has only to refer to Jacques Monod as opposed to Teilhard de Chardin and Whitehead. Nevertheless, the fact remains that it is suffering that resists an affirmative theory of the reconciliation of man and nature. Any attempt of that kind ultimately degenerates into a poverty-stricken kind of ontologization of human torment. Suffering emphasizes the contrast between nature and history, teleology and eschatology. There is no "objective" reconciliation between them, no obvious, manageable unity. All such attempts fall below the level of dignity of human suffering. This is especially clear in the case of the attempt to understand human suffering as a modality of a general interaction in nature between "action" and "passion". This, in both senses of the word, is nothing but a scholasticism of suffering. The least trace of meaningless suffering in the world we experience cancels all affirmative ontology and all teleology as untrue, and exposes them as a mythology of modern times (cf. Theodor Adorno).

Ultimately, human suffering resists all attempts to interpret history and historical processes in terms of nature, or to interpret nature as the subject of these historical processes. Of course, there is presupposed here that in this suffering we have a permanent, negative revelation of a consciousness of identity that cannot be reduced to the trivial identity of chronological inertia. This consciousness of identity does not mean the anthropocentrism of power and domination over nature, but an anthropocentrism of suffering which prevails against every form of cosmocentrism. It is not idealistic pride but respect for the dignity of the suffering accumulated in history that persuades us to try to understand nature from the viewpoint of history (which means interpreting the association between nature and history dialectically and not teleologically) and to interpret the thousands of millions of years of natural time as an "inflation time" compared with the historical time of suffering humanity (cf. Ernst Bloch).

Consequently, the substrate of human history is not nature as

[2] The background indicated in note 1 above is especially important for the understanding of the passage.

development or as a kind of process without any subject. The natural history of man is in a certain sense the history of his passion. In this sense, the lack of reconciliation between nature and man is not suppressed but maintained—in the face of all teleological projection and all ontological generalization. This history of passion has no goal, but—at most—a future. And a continuity of this history is made available to us not by means of teleology but—at most—by the "trace of suffering". The essential dynamics of history is accordingly the memory of suffering as a negative consciousness of future freedom and as a stimulus (with this freedom in our sights) to act to conquer suffering.

3. Christian faith declares itself as the *memoria passionis, mortis et resurrectionis Jesu Christi*. At the midpoint of this faith is a specific *memoria passionis*, on which is grounded the promise of future freedom for all. We remember the future of our freedom in the memory of this his suffering—this is an eschatological statement that cannot be made more plausible through any subsequent accommodation, and cannot be generally verified. This statement remains controversial and controvertible: the power to scandalize is part of its communicable content. For the truth of the passion of Jesus and the history of human suffering as we remember it in the word "God" is a truth whose recollection always painfully contradicts the expectations of the individual who tries to conceive it. The eschatological truth of the *memoria passionis* cannot be derived from our historical, social and psychological suasions. This is what makes it a liberating truth in the first place. But that also is at the root of its nature as constitutionally alien to our cognitive systems. If the eschatological truth of the *memoria passionis* is not merely to be expressed in empty tautologies and paradoxes, then it must be reflected upon within, and determined by, temporal circumstances, the memory of the suffering of Jesus must be deciphered as a subversively liberating memory within the apparent plausibilities of our society, and the christological dogmas must hold good as subversive formulas of that memory.

In this sense, the Christian *memoria* insists that the history of human suffering is not merely part of the pre-history of freedom but remains an inner aspect of *the* history of freedom. The imagination of future freedom is nourished from the memory of suffering, and freedom degenerates wherever those who suffer are treated more or less as a cliché and degraded to a faceless mass. Hence the Christian *memoria* becomes a "subversive remembrance", which shocks us out of ever becoming prematurely reconciled to the "facts" and "trends" of our technological society. It becomes a liberating memory over against the controls and mechanisms of the dominant consciousness and its abstract ideal of emancipation. The Christian *memoria passionis* articulates itself as a memory which makes one free to suffer from the sufferings of others, and to respect the prophetic witness of other's suffering, even though the negative view of suffering in our "progressive" society makes it appear as something increasingly intolerable and even repugnant. A society which suppresses these and similar dimensions in the history of freedom, and in the understanding of freedom, pays the price of an increasing loss of all visible freedom. It is incapable of developing goals and priorities which prevent the creeping adaptation of our freedom to the anonymous, impersonal framework of a computer society.

I should like to make two explanatory additions to the foregoing interpretation.

(*a*) It might well be objected that in this approach Christian memory is unilaterally reduced to the status of remembrance of suffering, and that the *memory of the resurrection of Jesus* is put into the background, if not altogether obscured. Obviously it is impossible to make a simple distinction between the *memoria passionis* and *memoria resurrectionis*. There is no understanding of the resurrection that does not have to be developed by way of and beyond the memory of suffering. There is no understanding of the joyousness of resurrection that is free of the shadows and threats of the human history of suffering. A *memoria resurrectionis* that would not be comprehensible as *memoria passionis* would be mythology pure and simple. But what of a *memoria passionis* which understands itself in faith as *memoria resurrectionis*? What does it mean to make "resurrection" accessible by way of the memory of suffering? Can such a resurrection faith also be expressed in socially communicable symbols which possess some critically liberating force for us? I believe that such a resurrection faith is expressed inasmuch as it acts "contra-factually" in making us free to bear in mind the sufferings and hopes of the past and the challenge of the dead. It allows not only a "for-ward-looking solidarity" (Walter Benjamin: with the "happiness of our grandchildren"), but a "backward-looking solidarity" (Benjamin: with the "suffering of our forefathers"). It allows not only a revolution that will change the things of tomorrow for future generations, but a revolution that will decide anew the meaning of our dead and their hopes. Resurrection mediated by way of the memory of suffering means: The dead, those already vanquished and forgotten, have a meaning which is as yet un-realized. The potential meaning of our history does not depend only on the survivors, the successful and those who make it. The history that we write and study in our history books is, in con-trast, almost always a "history of the victors", a history of those who made it, of the successful, of the people who got there. They never seem to mention the vanquished and the oppressed, the forgotten and suppressed hopes of our historical existence. But is that really so understandable? Why should the "right of the stronger"—a kind of historical Darwinism—prevail in history too? Great literature, on the other hand, has always tried in tragedies to search out the continuity and meaning of history in precisely the suppressed and buried "traces of suffering", to in-quire after the forgotten and unsuccessful ones of history, and in this way to write a kind of anti-history. This must be taken into account by a church and a theology where the "memory of suf-fering" occupies a central position. Only then will they be able to prevent themselves degenerating to the level of a church or a theology of the victors, and therefore of political religion (in something like the Constantinian sense). On the other hand, faith in the resurrection of the dead has a wholly social and social-critical significance. It enables us to insist firmly on the memory of the suffering that has accumulated in history, in order thereby to determine our behaviour and our hopes. Such an understand-ing of the unity of the *memoria passionis* and *memoria resur-rectionis* is also opposed to the attempt to make the conventional distinction between a this-worldly history of suffering and a supra-mundane history of glory: in fact, between world history and sacred history. World history and sacred history are neither two quantities which can be, so to speak, superficially equated by means of theological speculation, nor can they (nor ought they to) be merely formally contrasted. Sacred history is, instead, world history in which a meaning is conceded to obscured and suppressed hopes and sufferings. Sacred history is that world history in which the vanquished and forgotten possibilities of human existence that we call "death" are allowed a meaning which is not recalled or cancelled by the future course of history.

(b) We must also determine more precisely what is actually understood as "suffering" in the context of this article. Which "suffering", then, is intended in the *memoria passionis*? Isn't it very dangerous to talk about "suffering in general"? Doesn't the "memory of suffering" lose then all its critical, and above all its social-critical and political force? Doesn't that mean that suffering is wholly privatized and internalized? Doesn't everyone suffer, in a certain sense, in this view? Doesn't a rich playboy in his luxury bungalow suffer? Where are the requisite differentiations, the bases of a critical awareness in the interest precisely of those who suffer and are oppressed unjustly? Doesn't this lead to the entry of political commitment into the boring, non-specific vagueness which is for the most part the today of the social and political countenance of the world Church? Surely everything tends then towards that kind of consolation that ultimately consoles no one, since it intends exactly the same consolation for all. No! In the light of the Christian memory of suffering, it is clear that social power and political domination are not simply to be taken for granted but that they continually have to justify themselves in view of actual suffering. This is perhaps the only but the decisive political proposition that can be derived from the New Testament and its "theology of suffering". But it suffices. The social and political power of the rich and the rulers must be open to the question of the extent to which it causes suffering. It cannot escape this reckoning by invoking the specific suffering of the rich and powerful. And this critical interrogation of domination and riches is part precisely of that consolation which the Gospel would bestow upon the rich and the rulers. But this also means: I cannot overlook the suffering and oppression brought about by power and riches, and I cannot point out that the rich and powerful are also basically lonely and unhappy, and have their own form of suffering. I have instead the primary duty of opposing them, and this is a resistance which means that I confront them with the claim of Christian consolation and Christian redemption. The memory of suffering in the Christian sense does not, therefore, merge with the darkness of social and political arbitrariness, but creates a social and political conscience in the interest of others' suffering. It prevents the privatization and internalization of suffering, and the reduction of its social and political dimension.

4. As a kind of initial thesis, I suggested that the problem of the future was primarily political and fundamentally social. I now ask: How is the Christian *memoria passionis* to be connected at all with political life, and what justification is there for such an association? What have the two really got to do with one another? Doesn't bringing them together mean their mutual decay? As I have stressed, it is not a question here of a subsequent introduction of the Christian memory of suffering into the existing forms of political life, but of making this *memoria passionis* effective in the transformation of our political life and its structures—a transformation already shown to be the decisive requirement for tackling the question of the future. Yet the fundamental question remains: Doesn't political life fall victim to the reactionary influence of universalist norms once it is associated with the Christian *memoria passionis*? For this Christian *memoria*, as an eschatological remembrance, does entail a particular interpretation of the meaning and subject of universal history.

But how can the question of the meaning and subject of history as a whole have anything to do with political life? Doesn't all talk of a universal meaning of history in its political application lead to totalitarianism or, anyway, to an uncritical, fanatical kind of utopianism? All *positivist* theories of social and political life insist on this danger. These theories are, of course, subject to the question of whether their rigorous rejection of the question of meaning does not eventually subject political life to a purely instrumental form of thinking, and in the long run abandon it to technocracy. And positivism is also subject to the question of whether by its rendering taboo, or just ignoring, the question of meaning, it does not close its eyes to those ideologies which constantly seek to enthrone themselves as the subject and bearer of the meaning of history as a whole, and consequently endanger our social and political action.

In contrast, *traditional Marxism* and its theory of political life wholly maintain the question of the meaning and subject of history as a whole. The intention here is essentially practical: to determine the content and goal of revolutionary praxis. For Marxism does acknowledge a politically identifiable bearer of the meaning of history: and recognizes it as the proletariat, which in its political praxis sets out to realize this meaning. But in fact it is difficult to see how such a fusion of the meaning of history and political praxis doesn't eventually end in a political totalitarianism behind that transformation of political life that we seek for the sake of our future.

In its *"liberal"* theory of political life, traditional idealism also preserves the question of the meaning and subject of history. This position, however, differs from Marxism in acknowledging no socially apparent and politically identifiable subject of history as a whole, and, indeed, in rejecting any attempt at a political identification of this subject. Hegel, for instance, calls the subject of history as a whole the "world spirit", whereas others speak of "nature", and yet others of "universal humanity". These are all apolitical predicates. Here reference to the bearer and meaning of history remains essentially abstract. Nevertheless, it is clear that this abstract discourse about history as a whole can have an eminently practical political meaning. It makes possible and helps to bring about the liberation of political life from universal forces and universalist norms. Political life is set free to assume a wholly pragmatic orientation; politics as determined solely by the "thing itself"—what is "really at issue". But are these "factual structures" really anything other than the actual structures and tendencies of our economico-technological processes? Where are we to find a contra-factistic consciousness offering a political alternative to these processes and their anonymity, if not in a pure decision-politics? Undoubtedly its anti-totalitarian effect is important in this liberal understanding of political life; nevertheless, in its positive version it seems to offer no impulsion for the transformation of political life that we are looking for.

Let us look again at the association between the Christian *memoria passionis* and political life. In the memory of this suf-

fering, God appears in his eschatological freedom as the subject
and meaning of history as a whole. This implies, first of all, that
for this *memoria* there is also no politically identifiable subject
of universal history. The meaning and goal of this history as a
whole are instead—to put it very summarily—under the so-called
"eschatological proviso of God". The Christian *memoria* recalls
the God of Jesus' passion as the subject of the universal history
of suffering, and in the same movement refuses to give political
shape to this subject and enthrone it politically. Wherever a
party, group, race, nation, or class—even the class of technocrats
—tries to define itself as this subject, the Christian *memoria* must
oppose that, and unmask this attempt as political idolatry, as
political ideology with a totalitarian or—in apocalyptic term—a
"bestial" tendency. In this way, in the light of the Christian
*memoria passionis*, political life is liberated as protected from
totalitarianism. But, as opposed to the liberal version of idealism,
this liberation is now utopian in orientation and not undefined.
The Christian memory of suffering is in its theological implications an anticipatory memory: it intends the anticipation of a
particular future of man as a future for the suffering, the hopeless, the oppressed, the injured and the useless of this earth.
Hence this memory of suffering does not indifferently surrender
the political life oriented by it to the play of social interests and
forces, which for its own part turns upon the presupposition of
conflict, so that it always favours the powerful but not the
friendly, and always acknowledges only that measure of
humanity which is the estimated prerequisite for the successful
pursuit of one's own interests. The memory of suffering, on the
other hand, brings a new moral imagination into political life, a
new vision of others' suffering which should mature into a gen-
erous, uncalculating partisanship on behalf of the weak and un-
represented. Hence the Christian memory of suffering can become, alongside many other often subversive innovative factors
in our society, the ferment for that new political life we are seeking on behalf of our future.

5. Finally, let us consider the situation of the Churches in our
society. Clearly the Churches are now fast ceasing to be religious
establishments serving society as a whole; clearly they are increasingly becoming minorities, whose actual and public in-

fluence is constantly decreasing. They are becoming more and more what might well be termed cognitive and emotional minorities. The question arises whether the Churches are on the way to becoming sects. If the answer is Yes, are they to be more or less irrelevant subcultures within the framework of our technological super-society. This is the focal point of a number of questions that cannot be taken further here. I shall mention only one. *If* the Church spells out the *memoria passionis Jesu Christi* in the midst of our society—that memory of suffering in which the history of human passion is made unforgettable—then it can ultimately be or become a minority without necessarily falling into false sectarian self-seclusion. Then it will remain the bearer of a dangerous and subversive memory on which much more depends than the will to self-assertion of a religious institution—and that more is the future of our humanity.

*Translated by John Griffiths*

# Jürgen Moltmann

# The "Crucified God":
# God and the Trinity Today

THE debate about the existence of God and the function of faith has given rise in recent years to a feeling of uncertainty among Christians, who are moving, without much sense of direction, between the two poles of "God is dead" and "God cannot die". In struggling to renew the Church and to recreate society, many Christians have simply excluded the God question. Behind this political and social crisis in the Church, however, are the christological crisis—to whom do Christians ultimately refer their faith? —and the whole question of God—on which God is Christianity ultimately based, the crucified God or the idols of religion, class and race? The Church cannot be credible unless the Christian faith is certain. One of the consequences of this debate, however, has been a new convergence in theological thinking in the different Christian confessions, especially in the sphere of the doctrine of God.[1] I should like to discuss some aspects of this tendency in this article.

## I

Theological thinking about the God question has, of course, followed the suffering experienced by Christians because of injustice in the world and isolation in that suffering. History has

[1] H. Urs von Balthasar, "Mysterium Paschale", in *Mysterium Salutis* III, 2, pp. 133 ff.; H. Küng, *Menschwerdung Gottes. Eine Einführung in Hegels theologisches Denken als Prolegomena zu einer zukünftigen Christologie*, 1970; H. Mühlen, *Die Veränderlichkeit Gottes als Horizont einer zukünftigen Christologie*, 1969; E. Jüngel, "Vom Tod des lebendigen Gottes", in *ZThK* (1968), pp. 93–110; H. C. Geyer, "Atheismus und Christentum", in *EvTh* (1970), pp. 255–74.

26

concentrated for the most part on man's struggles for power and on class and racial struggles. If we are to find a universal history of man, we must look beyond these to the "history of suffering in the world".[2] Men are separated from their fellow men in possessing, in the positive aspects of life, but they are equal in poverty, in the negative aspects. Man's experience of suffering in the world goes beyond theism and atheism. It makes it impossible for him to believe in the existence of an omnipotent God who is good to all men and who "rules the world splendidly". A faith in God which justifies suffering and injustice in the world and does not protest against it is inhuman and even satanic in its effects. On the other hand, however, any protest against injustice tends to lose its impetus when it is based on atheism and a conviction that this world is the ultimate reality. The angry cry of protest is sustained by man's longing for the One who is completely different. As Max Horkheimer said, this is a "longing that the murderer will not triumph over the innocent victim".[3] It is a longing for justice in the world and for the One who ultimately guarantees it, and without this longing there can be no conscious suffering because of injustice. If man, suffering because of injustice, calls the existence of a just God into question, then the reverse also happens and his longing for justice and for the One who guarantees it causes him to question his suffering, so that it becomes a conscious pain. Suffering and protest go beyond theism and atheism to the question of theodicy: if God is just, what is the origin of evil? If the sting in the question "Why is there suffering?" is "God", then the sting in the question, "Is there a God?" is, of course, "suffering".

The traditional theistic answer to this twofold question is that this world is "God's world", a reflection of the deity, but the mirror is broken; the answer is no longer satisfying and strikes men as purely idolatrous. The traditional atheistic answer to this question simply deprives it of its foundation—as Stendhal and Nietzsche observed, "the only excuse for God is that he does not exist". What is ironical is that the non-existence of God is made into an excuse for God on the basis of a failed creation, which in

---

[2] W. Benjamin, *Ursprung des deutschen Trauerspiels* (1963), p. 183.
[3] M. Horkheimer, *Die Sehnsucht nach dem ganz Anderen. Ein Interview mit Kommentar von H. Gumnior* (1970), pp. 56 ff.

practice amounts to this—if man loses the habit of asking about justice, he will become adapted to and satisfied with bad relationships.

Critical Christians and critical atheists do, however, achieve a measure of agreement in the practical struggle against injustice within the context of the question of justice in the history of suffering in the world. But what does our recollection of the suffering of Christ mean for us in this context? Before we can answer this question, we have to find out the meaning of Christ's suffering first for God himself and then for the Christian believer. Since a God who reigns in a state of impartial blessedness in heaven cannot be accepted today, Christian theologians may have to reconsider the old theopaschitic questions. Did God suffer himself? Would a God who was incapable of suffering not be a God incapable of love and therefore poorer than any man? What meaning can a suffering God have for suffering men, on the other hand, apart from a religious confirmation of their suffering?

Theologians have to confront Christ's suffering and recognize God's being in Christ's crucifixion before they can deal with the question of suffering in the world without falling into Christian illusions on the one hand and atheistic resignation on the other. It is only when they are clear about what took place between the dying Jesus and "his" God that they will learn what this God means for those who suffer and are abandoned in the world.

## II

Of what did Jesus die? The Jews sentenced him on a charge of blasphemy because of his message of God's justice and unity with those deprived of all rights. The Romans crucified him because he threatened the *Pax Romana* and its gods. He died abandoned by the God and Father to whose coming he bore such striking witness in word and deed. Ultimately, then, Jesus died of his God and Father, who abandoned him. It is on this point, at which the Son of God is abandoned by the Father, that the question of God and suffering is concentrated.

One of the earliest testimonies is provided by Mark; according to this gospel, Jesus did not die bravely and beautifully, but crying out and weeping (Mark 15. 37). According to Mark 15. 34, he uttered the opening words of Ps. 22 ("My God, my God, why hast thou forsaken me?") and to complete the paradox, the centurion who had witnessed Jesus' death replied to this cry of abandonment by God by confessing that Jesus was the Son of God. How are we to interpret this? Obviously, the later tradition was offended by Mark's interpretation and reproduced Jesus' dying cry with more pious words. Various Western texts contain the version: "My God, with what do you reproach me?" and Luke has replaced the expression of Jesus' abandonment by words from the Jewish evening prayer from Ps. 31: 5: "Into thy hands I commend my spirit". For theological reasons, John said: "It is finished" (John 19. 30). We may, I think, assume that Mark's difficult version comes closest to the historical reality.

If two texts say the same thing, it does not have to mean the same in each case. It would therefore be wrong to interpret Jesus' cry from the cross in the sense of Ps. 22, but right to interpret the psalm in Jesus' sense.[4] "My God" in Ps. 22 is the God of the covenant with Israel and "I" is the suffering righteous man who presses God for his legal right of faithfulness under the covenant. In Jesus' use of "my God", on the other hand, there is the whole content of his new message of the approaching kingdom of God and of his own life led in closeness to God, which has enabled him to speak so exclusively about "my Father". This gives Jesus' abandonment a very distinctive aspect—the one who has abandoned him is not simply the God of the covenant with Israel, but his God and Father. Consequently the "I" who is abandoned is not simply the partner in the covenant, but the Son.

All the same, the legal nature of the complaint is full preserved. Jesus' cry from the cross has, like the psalmist's cry, nothing to do with despair—it is a call for God's faithfulness. Whereas the psalmist claims the righteous man's legal right to God's faithfulness under the covenant, Jesus claims his legal right as the Son to unity with his Father. Jesus' death means that not only God's faithfulness, but also the very deity of God, whose closeness and fatherhood Jesus had proclaimed, are at stake. This is why Jesus, in using these words, is claiming his

[4] See H. Gese, "Psalm 22 und das Neue Testament", ZThK (1968), pp. 1–22.

right to be in a special relationship with the Father, a relationship in which he is the Son. He is, in other words, saying: "My God, my God, why hast thou forsaken yourself?" This abandonment on the cross has therefore to be seen as something taking place between Jesus and his God and, there consequently, as taking place between God and God.

Why was Jesus' abandonment by God on the cross traditionally handed down at all after the Easter event? Clearly, there was an initial enthusiasm in the early Church, in which the cross represented no more than a transitional stage on the way to the glory which the primitive Christians experienced in the presence of the Spirit. Paul and Mark corrected this early Christian enthusiasm for the glorified Lord by calling to mind the lasting significance of the cross of Christ. They were convinced that, by penetrating further and further into the suffering of the unredeemed world, faith would discover more and more the real meaning of the crucifixion of the eschatological person of Christ. The resurrection of Christ did not reduce the cross to the level of a purely transitional stage. On the contrary, it raised it to the level of a saving event. The cross can be seen as a theological mystery not in the light of history, but only in the light of faith in the resurrection. In the history of man, after all, many prophets ended in the same way as Jesus. The Pauline and Marcan theology of the cross presupposes, in other words, faith in the Easter event. But how is it possible for God himself to be abandoned in his Son, to suffer and die in him?

### III

This poses a great dilemma for Christian theologians; indeed, both Catholics and Protestants who have specialized in the history of dogma are agreed that the *derelictio Jesu*, the abandonment of Jesus, was the central difficulty in the christology of the early Church. There was, it is true, a "religion of the cross" in the early Church's veneration of the crucified Christ. Ignatius was able to speak of the "sufferings of my God" (Rom. 6. 3) and to imitate them in his martyrdom. The theologians of the period were not, however, capable of identifying God's being with the suffering and death of Jesus, because of their fundamentally ancient concept of God, according to which God was incapable of suffering and dying, in contrast with man, who could suffer and die. Again, according to the ancient world, salvation was to be found in deification, which in turn meant immortality. Even Cyril of Alexandria, the early Christian Father who stressed most strongly the unity of divinity and humanity in Christ, felt bound to interpret the suffering and abandonment of Jesus as man's distress, not his own. Anyone who claims that Christ himself was overcome by fear and weakness is denying his divinity.[5] But was it really not possible in the early Church to relate Jesus' suffering to God's being?

The Council of Nicaea rightly declared, in opposition to Arius, that God was not so changeable as his creature. This is not an absolute statement about God, but a comparative statement. God is not subject to compulsion by what is not divine. This does not mean, however, that God is not free to change himself or to be changed by something else. We cannot deduce from the relative statement of Nicaea that God is unchangeable that he is absolutely unchangeable.

The early Fathers insisted on God's inability to suffer in opposition to the Syrian Monophysite heresy. An essential inability to suffer was the only contrast to passive suffering recognized in the early Church. There is, however, a third form of suffering—active suffering, the suffering of love, a voluntary openness to the possibility of being affected by outside influences. If God were really incapable of suffering, he would also be as incapable of loving as the God of Aristotle, who was loved by all, but could not love. Whoever is capable of love is also capable of suffering, because he is open to the suffering that love brings with it, although he is always able to surmount that suffering because of love. God does not suffer, like his creature, because his being is incomplete. He loves from the fullness of his being and suffers because of his full and free love.

The distinctions that have been made in theology between God's and man's being are externally important, but they tell us nothing about the inner relationship between God the Father and God the Son and therefore cannot be applied to the event of

---

[5] W. Elert, *Der Ausgang der altkirchlichen Christologie* (1957), p. 95.

the cross which took place between God and God. Christian humanists also find this a profound *aporia*. In regarding Jesus as God's perfect man, and in taking his exemplary sinlessness as proof of his "permanently powerful consciousness of God", they interpret Jesus' death as the fulfilment of his obedience or faith, not as his being abandoned by God. God's incapacity, because of his divine nature, to suffer (*apatheia*) is replaced by the unshakeable steadfastness (*ataraxia*) of Jesus' consciousness of God. The ancient teaching that God is unchangeable is thus transferred to Jesus' "inner life", but the *aporia* is not overcome. Finally, atheistic humanists who are interested in Jesus but do not accept the existence of God find it impossible to think of Jesus as dying abandoned by God and therefore regard his cry to God from the cross as superfluous.

All Christian theologians of every period and inclination try to answer the question of Jesus' cry from the cross and to say, consciously or unconsciously, why God abandoned him. Atheists also attempt to answer this question in such a way that, by depriving it of its foundation, they can easily dismiss it. But Jesus' cry from the cross is greater than even the most convincing Christian answer. Theologians can only point to the coming of God, who is the only answer to this question.

## IV

Christians have to speak about God in the presence of Jesus' abandonment by God on the cross, which can provide the only complete justification of their theology. The cross is either the Christian end of all theology or it is the beginning of a specifically Christian theology. When theologians speak about God on the cross of Christ, this inevitably becomes a trinitarian debate about the "story of God" which is quite distinct from all monotheism, polytheism or pantheism. The central position occupied by the crucified Christ is the specifically Christian element in the history of the world and the doctrine of the Trinity is the specifically Christian element in the doctrine of God. Both are very closely connected. "It is not the bare trinitarian formulas in the New Testament, but the constant testimony of the cross which provides the basis for Christian faith in the Trinity. The most concise expression of the Trinity is God's action on the cross, in which God allowed the Son to sacrifice himself through the Spirit."[6]

It is informative to examine Paul's statements about Jesus' abandonment on the cross in this context. The Greek word for "abandon" (*paradidomi*) has a decidedly negative connotation in the gospel stories of the passion, meaning betray, deliver, "give up" and even kill. In Paul (Rom. 1. 18 ff.), this negative meaning of *paredōken* is apparent in his presentation of God's abandonment of ungodly men. Guilt and punishment are closely connected and men who abandon God are abandoned by him and "given" up to the way they have chosen for themselves—Jews to their law, Gentiles to the worship of their idols and both to death.

Paul introduced a new meaning into the term *paredōken* when he presented Jesus' abandonment by God not in the historical context of his life, but in the eschatological context of faith. God "did not spare his own Son, but gave him up for us all; will he not also give us all things with him?" (Rom. 8. 32). In the historical abandonment of the crucified Christ by the Father, Paul perceived the eschatological abandonment or "giving up" of the Son by the Father for the sake of "ungodly" men who had abandoned and been abandoned by God. In stressing that God had given up "his own Son", Paul extended the abandonment of the Son to the Father, although not in the same way, as the Patripassian heretics had done, insisting that the Son's sufferings could be predicated of the Father. In the Pauline view, Jesus suffered death abandoned by God. The Father, on the other hand, suffered the death of his Son in the pain of his love. The Son was "given up" by the Father and the Father suffered his abandonment from the Son. Kazoh Kitamori has called this "the pain of God".[7]

The death of the Son is different from this "pain of God" the Father, and for this reason it is not possible to speak, as the Theopaschites did, of the "death of God". If we are to understand the story of Jesus' death abandoned by God as an event

[6] B. Steffen, *Das Dogma vom Kreuz. Beitrag zu einer staurozentrischen Theologie* (1920), p. 152.

[7] Kazoh Kitamori, *Theology of the Pain of God* (1965).

taking place between the Father and the Son, we must speak in terms of the Trinity and leave the universal concept of God aside, at least to begin with. In Gal. 2. 20, the word *paredōken* appears with Christ as the subject: "... the Son of God, who loved me and gave himself for me". According to this statement, then, it is not only the Father who gives the Son up, but the Son who gives himself up. This indicates that Jesus' will and that of the Father were the same at the point where Jesus was abandoned on the cross and they were completely separated. Paul himself interpreted Christ's being abandoned by God as love, and the same interpretation is found in John (John 3. 16). The author of 1 John regarded this event of love on the cross as the very existence of God himself; "God is love" (1 John 4. 16). This is why it was possible at a later period to speak, with reference to the cross, of *homoousia*, the Son and the Father being of one substance. In the cross, Jesus and his God are in the deepest sense separated by the Son's abandonment by the Father, yet at the same time they are in the most intimate sense united in this abandonment or "giving up". This is because this "giving up" proceeds from the event of the cross that takes place between the Father who abandons and the Son who is abandoned, and this "giving up" is none other than the Holy Spirit.

Any attempt to interpret the event of Jesus' crucifixion according to the doctrine of the two natures would result in a paradox, because of the concept of the one God and the one nature of God. On the cross, God calls to God and dies to God. Only in this place is God "dead" and yet not "dead". If all we have is the concept of one God, we are inevitably inclined to apply it to the Father and to relate the death exclusively to the human person of Jesus, so that the cross is "emptied" of its divinity. If, on the other hand, this concept of God is left aside, we have at once to speak of persons in the special relationship of this particular event, the Father as the one who abandons and "gives up" the Son, and the Son who is abandoned by the Father and who gives himself up. What proceeds from this event is the Spirit of abandonment and self-giving love who raises up abandoned men.

My interpretation of the death of Christ, then, is not as an event between God and man, but primarily as an event within the Trinity between Jesus and his Father, an event from which the Spirit proceeds. This interpretation opens up a number of perspectives. In the first place, it is possible to understand the crucifixion of Christ non-theistically. Secondly, the old dichotomy between the universal nature of God and the inner triune nature of God is overcome and, thirdly, the distinction between the immanent and the "economic" Trinity becomes superfluous.[8] It makes it necessary to speak about the Trinity in the context of the cross, and re-establishes it as a traditional doctrine. Seen in this light, this doctrine no longer has to be regarded as a divine mystery which is better venerated with silent respect than investigated too closely. It can be seen as the tersest way of expressing the story of Christ's passion. It preserves faith from monotheism and from atheism, because it keeps it close to the crucified Christ. It reveals the cross in God's being and God's being in the cross. The material principle of the trinitarian doctrine is the cross; the formal principle of the theology of the cross is the trinitarian doctrine. The unity of the Father, the Son and the Holy Spirit can be designated as "God". If we are to speak as Christians about God, then, we have to tell the story of Jesus as the story of God and to proclaim it as the historical event which took place between the Father, the Son and the Holy Spirit and which revealed who and what God is, not only for man, but in his very existence. This also means that God's being is historical and that he exists in history. The "story of God" then is the story of the history of man.

## V

In the history of Christianity, the God of the poor, the sick and the oppressed has always been the suffering, persecuted and oppressed Christ, whereas the God of the rich and ruling classes is and always has been the Pantokrator.[9] But what does the God

---

[8] K. Rahner, "Bemerkungen zum dogmatischen Traktat *De Trinitate*", in *Schriften zur Theologie*, IV, pp. 103–36.

[9] See, for example, N. Gorodeckaja, *The Humiliated Christ in Modern Russian Thought* (1938); J. Cone, "Singend mit dem Schwert in der Hand. Eine theologische Interpretation schwarzer Spirituals", *Ev. Komm.* (1971), pp. 442–7; H. Lüning, *Mit Maschinengewehr und Kreuz—oder wie kann das Christentum überleben?* (1971). These authors show how the piety of impotent and oppressed people, slaves, serfs and Indians, has been concentrated on the passion of Christ and the figure of the suffering God. Any theology of liberation has to begin with this form of christology.

who appears as the suffering servant, the suffering and crucified Son of Man mean for the history of human suffering in the world?

Anyone who suffers without apparent reason always thinks, at least at first, that he has been abandoned by God. If he calls out in suffering, he is calling out with Jesus on the cross. God is, in this case, not the one who is facing him but hidden from him, to whom he is calling, but the human God who is calling out with him and in him and who champions him with his cross at the point where he is silent in anguish. The suffering man does not simply protest against his fate. He suffers because he is alive and he is alive because he loves. The man who no longer loves no longer suffers. He has become indifferent to life. The more a man loves, the more vulnerable he becomes. The extent to which he is vulnerable depends on the extent to which he is capable of happiness and vice versa. This is a process which can be called the dialectic of human life. Love makes man alive and mortal. The aliveness of life and the mortality of death are qualities which man experiences in his interest in life, and this interest is what we call love.

The theistic God is poor. He cannot suffer because he cannot love. The protesting atheist loves, but in a despairing way. He is made to suffer because he loves, but he protests against his suffering and therefore against love, which caused him to suffer. How can a man continue to love despite disappointment and death? The faith which comes about as a result of the event of the cross does not answer the question of suffering either by giving a theistic explanation that it has to be like that or by making a gesture of protest against its being like that. On the contrary, the answer of faith is to lead despairing love back to its origin— "He who abides in love abides in God and God abides in him" (1 John 4. 16).

Wherever men suffer because they love, God suffers in them. God suffered Jesus' death and proved the strength of his love in that suffering. This same suffering enables men to find the strength to endure what threatens to annihilate them and to "seize death". Hegel called this seizing death "the life of the spirit, which is not a life that recoils from death and protects itself from devastation, but a life which endures death and preserves itself in it".[10] The man who loves and is made to suffer because of that love and therefore experiences the mortality of death inevitably enters the "story of God". If he recognizes that his abandonment is made to cease in Christ's abandonment by God, he can "abide in love" in communion with Christ's giving himself up.

Hegel believed that only a conscious knowledge of God as a Trinity made it possible for Christians to regard the cross of Christ as the "story of God": "This is for the community the story of God's appearance. This story is a divine story, through which the community has reached a conscious knowledge of the truth. This conscious knowledge that God is three in one has resulted from this. The reconciliation which Christians accept in Christ is meaningless if God is not known as the triune God."[11]

The event of the cross thus becomes, for the believer who loves, the story of God which reveals the future. In the present, this means reconciliation with the pain of love. In the future, it means love in a free world without anxiety and power. The history of suffering in the world is included in the "story of God" because of the story of Christ's suffering. As Whitehead has said, "In this sense, God is the great companion—the fellow sufferer, who understands". In the Trinity, God is both immanent in human history and transcendent. To use inadequate figurative language, he is transcendent as the Father, immanent as the Son and as the Spirit of history he reveals the future. If we understand God in this way, we shall be able to understand our own history, the history of man's suffering and hope, as the "story of the history of God". The history of life goes beyond theistic resignation and atheistic protest, because it is the history of man's interest in life, love.

*Translated by David Smith*

---

[10] Hegel, *Phänomenologie des Geistes, Werke* (ed. Glockner), 2, 34.
[11] Hegel, *Philosophie der Religion, Werke* (ed. Glockner), 16, 2, 308.

Norbert Schiffers

# Suffering in History

## I. The Prospect for the Hopeless Sufferer is Nothingness

SUFFERING is not a human experience, mode of behaviour or task to which man can turn whenever he wants to, or from which he can escape in his free time. All men have a time for thinking, working, committing themselves, reading and writing, laughing and crying. These are not necessarily everyday activities and everyone can dissociate himself from them so as to renew his strength and then recommit himself to creative work.

Suffering man is in a different position. By "suffering man", I do not mean someone who is listless, morose or bitter at times, but someone whose suffering is so acute and long-lasting that he feels powerless to break away from it. Such a man is held captive by his suffering and experiences a total loss of freedom. He may even reach the point where he is so accustomed to suffering that he becomes indifferent to it, as indifferent as he is to life itself, where he succumbs to the terrible experience of accepting a kind of peace in hopelessness. It is impossible, however, to rest in this hopeless peace. There seems to be no way of dealing with the present or of approaching the future in this state. The future, indeed, does not exist for suffering man. The prospect for the hopeless sufferer is nothingness.

This nothingness is first seen as a blurring of all outlines. Time and space become nebulous, but the sufferer believes that he can still feel his way along these vague outlines. As soon as he tries to free himself, however, by drawing aside the veil of his grief, he finds that he can no longer grasp hold of any word, idea or image. There is no way ahead—on every side, above and below him, before him and behind him, there is nothing but a vague space without direction or aim. Yet even this space, in which the sufferer finds himself and out of which he cannot feel his way, is not a true space. It is simply nothingness. It is a nothingness which is everywhere identical and indifferent. Nothing stands out in opposition to it and nowhere is the word of peace, patient waiting, feeling and watching heard. In this infinite void, there is only a state of suspense, in which man is like a dead and weightless object.

In his vision of the dead and suspended Christ in the empty building of the world, the German Romantic Jean Paul presented the terror of suffering in the boundless void outside time and space, the terror of nothingness, a nothingness that is always and everywhere the same and always indifferent. Although his vision is no more, one might say, than a poet's image, it is undeniably an extremely graphic presentation of the state of suffering man. The hell of the sufferer is to be aimless and weightless and as dead as a lifeless object.

## II. The Traces of Suffering are Weak Images of Everyday Experience which are Strong Enough to Deny Nothingness

It is probable that Jean Paul saved himself from the terror of nothingness and the void by his vision of this weightless, meaningless state at the end of suffering. Even by representing it in this way as the image of a dead spectre, he replaced nothingness, the void, by anxiety, by fear. Anxiety enables impending disaster to be experienced as a weight which the suffering man who has little hope can try to oppose. When he began to feel the approach of mental disorder, van Gogh saw himself in this way and painted himself as an ageing man with an untidy beard and red-rimmed eyes on a stool. Bending forward, half collapsed, he was still able to support himself (in this self-portrait), with his arms on his knees and still able to raise himself a little. The man thus drawn with the traces of suffering seems to be looking for what is ordinary, the stool and his limbs, to support himself and even to lift himself up.

The man who really suffers can, by writing or painting, have a vision of nothingness without an object and thus enter an object which will deny nothingness. In this way, Jean Paul created his vision as an image of the dead Christ hanging in a void. Van Gogh painted a self-portrait in which the spatial diagonals of a stool were opposed to nothingness. Stefan Andres, in his *We are Utopia*, described how a spot of damp on the ceiling above the bed of a suffering man became for that man the outline map of the land he longed for, Utopia. In Psalm 107, the cry of the oppressed, whom no one can support any more, sounds through the deathlike darkness of the desert, and metal gates, iron bars and chains become the signposts directing those who have lost their way in nothingness.

The everyday experience that mental disturbance is not synonymous with the onset of infinite nothingness thus becomes an image against nothingness for disoriented, suffering man. Walls enclosing prison cells in which men crouch impotent in prayer on the ground, listening for an answer, may serve as images against nothingness. The man who suffers so much that he sees himself slipping closer and closer into nothingness still fashions objects, utters cries and creates images against nothingness to protect himself from mental disorder. The suffering man even calls out when there is no one apart from himself to hear his cries, simply because he needs the echo of reality, not another, listening man. He tries to raise himself up and to find direction by using this image of the world and the echo of his own voice. The trace of suffering is therefore the trace of suffering man himself. It is the trace of the flickering candle, the trace of the fibre of root which may eventually become a tree. As André Malraux observed, the traces of suffering are weak images which are strong enough to deny our nothingness.

Whether these weak images, these wonders of denial enacted by man in protest against nothingness, are designed against the heavy darkness or against the brilliant light is of little importance. In his *Return to Tipasa*, Albert Camus has described how he exposed himself to the brilliant noonday sun in an attempt to quench his thirst for love and admiration. Struck by the light, however, he finds that admiration vanishes because unhappiness rises up from his dreams. "Looking at the sea...at midday," he writes, "I quench my double thirst for love and admiration.

If we are not loved, it is just bad luck. But if we do not love, it is unhappiness... O light, I learned at last, may there always be an unquenchable summer in me."

It would seem, then, that Camus sought the image of summer to combat the nothingness that spelt unhappiness. But this search was linked in his case with an unquenchable thirst for love and this introduces us to a new theme in the "trace of suffering"— the theme of melancholy.

## III. MELANCHOLY DENIES THE WEAK TRACES OF UPRIGHT MAN IN THE WORLD AND PREFERS THE STRONG IMAGE OF DESTRUCTIVE DEATH

It is the constant experience of the one who loves that he has not loved enough, so that, looking back, love becomes a weak trace making the lover suffer. The man who suffers because his love was inadequate, however, is always tempted to melancholy, which destroys any strong denial of nothingness. Melancholy, Camus believed, was man's unhappiness, making him look at nothingness, and thus incapable of denying that nothingness with ordinary everyday images. His reference to unquenchable love concerns the unhappiness that lies behind the happiness of admiration and rouses the sleeping lion of melancholy, because admiration is only the weak image of love which denies, with its unconditional affirmation, the nothingness. Something very similar is probably meant by Paul and the author of 1 John when they say that all men show a lack of love and this confronts man with death and makes him conscious of unhappiness, the life-destroying power of death. The song of love and suffering is only strong when its weak images of life do not slip imperceptibly into the melody of melancholy, which can only lament life.

Man's experience that his love is never enough can become pathos, a song of death, a pathological song of the melancholy of the one who loves. This pathos of brooding melancholy, caused by the knowledge that no one ever loves enough, is, as a trace of suffering, an expression of those who circle around the fact that they are never enough. The burden of human experience which insists that not even love is strong enough to change the world can alter man's experience and his denial of nothingness because it continues to be an experience of man's own weakness. If suffering man does not manage to find weak images of his own strength instead of an image of his own weakness, he will inevitably seek to end his suffering in death.

The loving man's increasingly concentrated experience that he can never love enough may become traces of suffering so material that they point straight to death. The strong images that man has of his love being never enough seldom remain weak traces of suffering because man has such a passion for thinking in straight lines. These images are purchased for the price which pathetically courts death as an escape from suffering. The melancholy man is ready to pay this price, and pays it willingly when he sees the weak images of the strong man in the traces of suffering. This is because he habitually denies what he sees, refusing to acknowledge the reality of the weak man and preferring the power of death as a sign of freely chosen strength.

## IV. REMEMBERING EVERYDAY EXPERIENCE MEANS RE-ORIENTING ONE'S LIFE BY THE TRACES OF SUFFERING

Those who express the weak traces of suffering in speech, poetry or art have a more honest attitude towards themselves and the realities of human existence than those neurotic victims of melancholy. They do not attempt to oppose the threat of nothingness by a conscious act of death. As men who suffer and are broken by action, they do not want to choose action again. These artists of the weak traces of suffering find that action—both their own and that of others—means further suffering and they consequently apply all the power of their rational minds to calling space to mind, space for a stool, for instance, in an attempt to overcome the timeless and spaceless quality of nothingness. They remember the square in Tipasa and the infinite yet limited spatial dimensions of the empty building of the world. They cling to the walls of their prison cells which echo their own cries in an effort to rediscover the world that has been lost in suffering. They use memory to lift themselves up and the world in which they live, in the hope that time and space will be recreated with whatever objects are available, in order to overcome nothingness and its consequences.

Those weakened by suffering turn memory into an experience of time and space in the remaining traces of suffering for their fellows who are tormented by nothingness. These traces become for them norms which change the void into the pathetic everyday experience that man so urgently needs if he is to continue to live. Remembering this everyday experience is equivalent to giving suffering a trace of life as a means of orientation. The remembered traces which confront nothingness with life are lines of orientation in time and space. They are traces of people who rediscover themselves and the story of their lives in the little, perhaps even the only thing that they still have. The traces of suffering, then, are the rediscovered traces of this story, the story of the suffering person himself.

V. The Traces of Suffering are the Personal Traces of the Sufferer himself; the Theory of Suffering, the Cult of the Hero and Sympathy are Falsifications, not Traces of Suffering

It is therefore possible to accept memory as the sufferer's means of raising himself up and the world he lives in and of overcoming melancholy and its deceptive consolation and the nothingness that threatens him in his suffering. In this case, however, we must, if we are to avoid misinterpretation examine critically the stories which those who suffer tell of themselves.

Older people often bore us with the intensity with which they tell again and again the same story of their youth. They repeat these remembered stories so often that one is inclined to suspect that they need to resist everything that threatens life and, when faced with death, look for refuge in the happiness of the past. This is not so, however. Older people, weakened by the experience of suffering, tell these stories to prove to themselves and to younger people that they too can exist in the present. Their memories help them to rediscover the confidence that assures them of everything they wanted and were able to do. They do not tell these stories with vanity and pride, but almost always with the underlying intention that everything that they could do, young people can do now and will do in the future. They tell these stories to restore their own confidence in themselves and at the same time to inspire confidence in those who listen to them in the power that governs life. Their remembrances of the past are not an attempt to seek flight. On the contrary, their real purpose is to show how it is possible to persevere in life.

Assuming that this interpretation is correct, we may go a stage further. In narrating past memories which point to a power governing life, these older people want to draw their fellow men away from the traces of suffering which they themselves have to bear. They know from their own experience that they have to bear this suffering themselves and cannot shake it off. They do not, however, want their fellow men to give their undivided attention to this personal suffering. This is why they try to divert them from it by their stories, which are fundamentally memories of power and strength in life.

If this argument is correct, we are made at once aware of the deepest reason why people who are threatened by suffering wish to draw the attention of others away from its traces. It is because they know from personal experience that their suffering and its traces are exclusively their own. They are not universally valid. Others cannot experience them in exactly the same way. No theory can be built up on them. Man's will to live and human hope—these are two virtues that can be experienced by all and converted into theories. Each man's suffering is such a unique experience that it is not communicable to others. It is indeed so frightening to them that it is better to divert their attention away from it to the power that governs life, the strength that all people can experience.

If this is true, then it is a real objection to the theologians' theory of suffering which claims to be a universally valid norm, but is based only on the suffering experienced by the individual and which, it is hoped, will trace a path from man to God. Those who theorize about suffering in fact obliterate the trace of suffering and issue counterfeit money when men ought rather to countersign the bill of suffering. Although this discovery is likely to annoy theorists who are looking for what is universally valid, necessary and absolute, it will at the same time foster respect for those who suffer, because suffering is such a unique experience that it protects the sufferer from the sympathy of his fellow men. As a desire for feeling, sympathy would perhaps succeed if it were possible to form a theory about the traces of suffering as a

venerating them as heroes, thus banishing them from our
world of everyday experience. As our world is nourished by the
realities to which suffering people cling, those people belong
us and should not be isolated and treated as if they were in
one way special. If the Romans had not come to worship their
emperors, they would undoubtedly have worshipped their own
god in the everyday environment of the home. Christians have
always insisted that the martyrs belong to the Church, which is
in turn embedded in the everyday experience of the world. Admittedly Jesus died outside the town, but he is venerated by
Christians in the everyday course of their lives, which are characterized by their everyday cross. There is nothing disrespectful
about this, because our world is so full of the traces of those who
suffer. In that world, only the cult of the exceptional man, the
hero, is painful. This brings us to the second aspect, indeed to
the second trace, the indirect trace of God which is present in
the traces of suffering.

## VI. God's Indirect Trace in the Traces of Human Suffering

It hardly needs to be proved, in an article on traces of suffering,
that neither these traces nor suffering itself are caused by God,
but that both are caused by man. It is nowhere stated in the Old
Testament, for example, that suffering is a constitutive characteristic of the people of God. Suffering came about in the world
of the Bible because of fathers, sons, relatives and enemies or because of situations such as catastrophes (2 Kings 22. 19), injustices
(Ezek. 35. 5), exploitation (Ezek. 18. 18), poverty (2 Cor. 8. 13),
persecution (1 Thess. 1. 6), imprisonment (Acts 20. 23) and so on.

The same applies to the traces of suffering in the Bible. Fear,
arising out of distress, brings a cry or a curse to man's lips, makes
him grope in the darkness for objects or for the hand of his
fellow man or makes him look forward to the dawn or the sun-
light (Job 17. 3, 12–16; Zeph. 1. 15–18; Isa. 8. 21 ff.; John 5. 7).
The traces of suffering, tears, sweat, blood and human cries—
—these cover the earth, but they are not the traces of God, but
the traces of Job, the traces of man (Job 16 and 17).

In the New Testament, this suffering is concentrated in the
man Jesus in such a way that the traces of suffering can be inter-

preted as the trace of Christ (Col. 1. 24; Phil. 3. 10; 1 Peter 4. 13; see also 2 Cor. 1. 5; 4. 8, 10 ff.; Rev. 7. 14).

According to the Bible, then, the traces of suffering in the world are always the traces of suffering man. They are not the traces of God or of God's pain concerning the world. We cannot use the Bible to raise man's suffering and the traces of that suffering to the level of heaven—they remain here on earth, under the altar, as an accusation against us (see Rev. 6. 9 ff.). Not poverty, distress, suffering or sorrow are called blessed, but the poor, the distressed, the suffering and the sorrowful—all those who leave the traces of their suffering in our world. People like the poor man Lazarus lie in front of our doors. They accuse us and at the same time they see God (Luke 16. 19 ff.).

This is all that the Bible tells us about God and human suffering—that God sees human suffering and the traces of that suffering, which are not his, but those of suffering people. They are, however, traces of suffering people who were looking for life and God sees them. This is why the Bible tells us that the time of suffering is the time of God's visitation and that the weak are the strong and the traces of suffering are the traces of Jesus' passion in the world, signs of accusation and judgment and signs of salvation in our world of everyday experience.

It is because God sees those who suffer and regards their traces as valuable that the traces of suffering are the direct traces of man and the indirect trace of God. This may seem too little to some of us, but we should remember that the traces of suffering can be found everywhere in our world as the traces of suffering people who raise themselves up against the nothingness. Those traces are there, moreover, as traces of judgment and of salvation, as signs and as the indirect trace of God.

*Translated by David Smith*

Gregory Baum

# Cultural Causes for the Change of the God Question

THE classical question of God dealt with his existence. "Is there a God? Is the visible universe all that is, or is there over and above the world an invisible, supreme being called God?" This was the crucial question people posed themselves, and—depending on their answer—they were either theists or atheists. Christians were theists: they believed and proclaimed God's existence as the basic presupposition of the Christian faith. But is there really this invisible supreme being? Philosophers over the centuries have examined this question and come up with contradictory conclusions: some thought that they could demonstrate God's existence from the existence of the things we see, while others thought they could render an account of the visible universe without any reference to the divine.

Today the crucial question about God has changed. At least, this is the contention of many contemporary theologians. Because of significant changes of Western society, which eventually even affected life in the Church, people have redefined their relationship to reality and thus come to pose the question about the divine in a new way. It is significant that for the first time in history God has become problematic within the Christian Church. But before we can formulate the contemporary question about God, we must look at the roots of man's new self-understanding in the social institutions of modern life and examine the role of religion in the making of society.

## I. The New Self-understanding

The change in modern man's self-awareness is rooted in two important historical events, the Industrial Revolution and the French Revolution. The social thinkers of the last century, whether conservative, liberal or radical, agreed on the crucial role of these two events: they often even agreed in their description (if not in their evaluation) of the modern consciousness then in the making.[1]

I shall summarize the effects of the two revolutions on society and consciousness. The Industrial Revolution introduced a new mobility into European society. The creation of large industrial centres drew labourers from the village communities, destroyed the traditional patterns of life, robbed the simple people of their inherited security, and created new cities, the centres of poverty and exploitation. At the same time the successful people in the new cities were free to create conditions of life according to their own ideals. For them the breakdown of traditional patterns meant new possibilities of controlling and transforming society. The creation of large industries enabled some people to acquire great wealth, rise on the social scale, and assume a new role of power in society. Both the horizontal and the vertical mobility in society undermined traditional values, deprived social life of its stability, and introduced a principle of ongoing social change.

In addition, the new technology associated with large-scale industrialization improved the material conditions of life among the bourgeoisie and created a desire for improving the standard of living every year. The conditions of life were no longer regarded as a fixed reality, to which men had to adapt: they were, rather, a task and a responsibility. People began to dream of creating living conditions according to their own choice.

In a similar way, the French Revolution modified the political imagination of Western man. The dramatic events that took place in France at the end of the eighteenth century convinced the people of the West that social institutions, however sacred and time-honoured they may have been, were not permanent; they were man-made and hence could be dismantled and rebuilt

[1] For references see, for example, R. Nisbet, *The Sociological Tradition* (New York, 1968).

according to a new vision. The ideal of democracy expressed the search for social institutions on all levels, corresponding to the values and purposes of the people who actually belonged to them. Here again society appeared not as a given reality, to which men must conform, but as a human task, a structure to be created, and a product of human life and action.

Whereas urbanization, social mobility, expanding technology and democratic structures at first affected people only at certain significant centres in Europe and America, the social thinkers of the nineteenth century clearly foresaw that these social institutions would spread throughout the entire West and eventually transform the consciousness of people on a vast scale. Needless to say, the roots of this new consciousness went back beyond the two revolutions mentioned above, which were, after all, the highpoints of preceding cultural and political developments. What the two revolutions did was to create social institutions that were to determine the forms of life of entire populations and thus initiate people into a new awareness of themselves and their environment.

This new consciousness was inevitably a reflection of men's actual experience of society. While at one time the social reality was a given for men, which they tried to understand and into which they tried to fit their lives, now reality was experienced as unfinished, as something that still had to be built, as a social process, the past of which was a given but the future of which was still undetermined and open to men's action. Reality came to be looked upon as a process, a development, an ongoing creation, which was not fully determined by static laws but passed through men's free decisions and activities. People began to feel responsible for their future. It was up to them, as a people, to build their world and by doing so to engage in their own self-transformation. Philosophers and sociologists, while using different conceptual tools, began to look upon human action as the crucial activity by which men constitute the world in which they live and, simultaneously, create themselves as a people. The thinkers who proposed this understanding of reality were convinced that this view was not a remote, overly intellectual construct, but that it expressed the awareness of ordinary people living under these new conditions. Unfinished man, unfinished reality—these were the given. The human task was to build reality and by so doing to create men as free and responsible beings.

With this awareness of reality it was inevitable that thinkers acquired a new appreciation of thought and knowledge. Man's mental activity was part of building the world. Truth was not a private achievement of the mind, consisting of the mind's conformity to a reality outside of it: truth came to be looked upon as an element, an essential element, in the production of the world and the ongoing self-constitution of man. Thought and action were more intimately connected than had been suspected in the past. In this perspective, religious truth also came to be understood in terms of the world which it created and the action of which it was an expression. This is the context in which the question of God acquired a new meaning.

## II. Religion and Ideology

While the philosophers of the Enlightenment had regarded religion as a cluster of superstition to be discarded, the new social thinkers of the nineteenth and the early twentieth centuries became aware of religion as a function in society. Even when their evaluation of religion was totally negative, as in the case of Karl Marx, they understood it as a significant expression of social life. Among the sociologists a positive evaluation of religion was very common. Emile Durkheim, for example, looked upon religion as the celebration of the social bond that constitutes a society.[2] Religion is the glue that keeps a society together. Religion creates and nourishes the values out of which people produce their social, cultural and personal life. Other sociologists, such as Max Weber, were more sensitive to the dynamic function of religion.[3] Since religion is a source of interiority and determines man's own self-definition, it has a unique potential for social criticism and social change. Here, too, religion is seen as one of the most powerful social forces. In this perspective, a religious statement expresses man's relationship to culture and society and gives rise to a par-

[2] Cf. E. Durkheim, *The Elementary Forms of Religious Life* (New York, 1965).
[3] Cf. M. Weber, *The Sociology of Religion* (Boston, 1968).

ticular course of action. Religion is part of building the world of
men.

The radical social thinkers, on the other hand, understood religion as the expression of man's alienation from his fellow men
and from nature. It was a symptom of social sickness, a reflection
of the structures of domination that estranged men from the
deepest level of their humanity. For Marx, religion was "the
sigh of the oppressed creature, the sentiment of a heartless world,
and the soul of soulless conditions.[4] Religion was an illusion produced by men's failure to recognize the actual social conditions
and power structures operative in their lives.

It is highly significant that Marx rejected the atheistic materialism of the philosophers of the Enlightenment, including Feuerbach, almost as much as he did religion.[5] Feuerbach had still
dealt with the classical God question: "Is there a God?" His
answer had been negative. Yet according to Marx, Feuerbach
had overlooked the social significance of religion. He had not
asked what it was in society, what sickness or what oppression,
that compelled people to create illusions for themselves. As long
as this question remained unasked and no effort was made to
change society, Marx held, people would remain in false consciousness and simply replace one illusion by another. Traditional
atheistic materialism was as much an ideology as religion, except
that it reflected the interests of a different class. Not every atheism
is true. Marx saw the religious question in a new light. The truth
of a religious statement depends on its weight and power in the
actual history of men. What consciousness does the religious
statement express and what action does it initiate?

While Marx's unqualified equation of religion and ideology is
wholly unacceptable, few people today would deny the ideological
component in religion and other cultural manifestations. Christians in particular have come to recognize that present in their
religion, in its doctrinal formulations, its liturgical expressions

---

[4] "Critique of Hegel's Philosophy of Right", *Karl Marx: Early Writings,*
ed. T. R. Bottomore and M. Rubel (New York and London, 1956),
pp. 43-4.
[5] Cf., especially, the famous "Theses on Feuerbach", *Karl Marx: Selected
Writings*, ed. T. R. Bottomore and M. Rubel (New York and London,
1956), pp. 67-9.

and its forms of organization, are elements of varying proportions that represent an unconscious defence of social privileges and political power. There is, first of all, the ideology of class, which Marx made central in his analysis. The close tie of an ecclesiastical institution to the dominant class in a society gives religion and the religious message a strong ideological thrust, protecting the political *status quo* and promoting the continuance of the present social order. Today the Christian can give many examples from his own country, from ecclesiastical life in Europe and America, and from the Church's mission on other continents, where the Church's close connection to a political party, possibly to an unjust social order, and even to a regime of oppression, has given the Christian message an ideological significance. There are situations where the proclamation of God is a defence of the established law and order and the message of the charity and suffering of Christ a hidden way of counselling patience and forbearance in the face of social injustice.

There is, moreover, the ideology of nation. Christians have become aware that intense national feeling can enter the very fibres of religion and thus find expression even in the practice and proclamation of the Gospel. Every nation tends to generate a kind of civil religion, a myth glorifying its national destiny, that easily merges with the religion of the Gospel.[6] Religion can become an expression of, and a disguise for, nationalistic sentiments. In many countries nationalistic groups become the vocal defenders of the rights of God and his Church. At the same time the Christian Churches tend to be rather insensitive to the failings and crimes of the nation to which they belong. What does the assurance that God exists mean in various historical situations?

Today we have become aware of the ideology of race and culture. Built into religion can be the claim of racial superiority and the protection of a particular cultural ideal. We have the curious phenomenon in several countries in Europe and America that agnostic or even atheistic citizens, deeply attached to the glory of their land or to the continuance of the inherited racial or cultural dominance, speak out against the doctrinal and liturgical changes

[6] Cf. R. N. Bellah, "Civil Religion in America", *The Religious Situation 1968*, ed. D. R. Cuttler (Boston, 1968), pp. 331–55.

taking place in the Catholic Church and the other Christian Churches.

Finally, there is the ideology of personal life, explored above all by depth psychology. While Freud's reductionist view of religion as unconscious projection due to the repression of the instincts is totally unacceptable, few people today would deny that present in religion are projections, of varying intensity and content, produced by unresolved instinctual problems possibly going back to early childhood. Especially priests and ministers who spend much time in personal counselling have become aware that many problems about God and salvation are not religious problems at all, but disguises for human problems that individuals refuse to face. Today even Christians who have no acute emotional problems search for greater self-knowledge and wish to discern in their faith and practice the elements of projection due to unconscious resistance against vital conflicts. Christians are quite willing to admit that religion can become the expression of false consciousness or a screen keeping a man away from seeing reality as it is.

At the same time Christians believe that the Gospel saves men from false consciousness. Jesus Christ has come to deliver men from their illusions and the power these illusions have over them. In his struggle against the powerful in Israel Jesus revealed how religion can become a hidden, largely unconscious defence of political power, and of social and national privileges. In his struggle against legalism, Jesus revealed how religion can become the source of deadly compulsion and repetitive action in people's lives, and alienate them from salvation. His promise was that his message would make people free. In the Gospel, we conclude, Christ revealed that religion, including the one preached in his name, is in need of an ongoing critique.

The preceding reflections have shown that Christians are no longer content to understand a religious statement, or a statement about God's existence, simply in conceptual terms: they also want to examine its actual weight and power in life and history. The identical statement about God does not necessarily have the same meaning on the tongues of various people. Christians must ask themselves what relationship to society and personal life a statement about God reflects and what action it promotes in the people who accept it. Not every theism is necessarily in keeping with the Gospel.[7] Theism is acceptable only to the extent that it is non-ideological. Theism is acceptable only to the extent that it expresses and promotes the reconciliation and elevation of mankind. The crucial question for vast numbers of people today is not the classical theistic question "Is there a God?", but how can our consciousness, personal and social, be so transformed that it expresses and promotes a relationship to life and society that is in harmony with the Gospel of Jesus Christ.

## III. THE QUESTION ABOUT THE DIVINE

The new awareness that reality is unfinished and man is called upon to create his own future has profoundly influenced the life of the Church in the twentieth century. Even religious statements are being understood as the expression of man's responsibility for human life and his hope for the destiny of mankind. The first time this new consciousness was officially acknowledged by the Catholic Church was at Vatican II: "In every group or nation, there is an ever-increasing number of men and women who are conscious that they themselves are the artisans and authors of their culture and their community. Throughout the world there is a similar growth in the combined sense of independence and responsibility. Such a development is of paramount importance for the spiritual and moral maturity of the human race. This truth grows clearer if we consider how the world is becoming united and how we have the duty to build a better world based on truth and justice. Thus we are witnesses of the birth of a new humanism, one in which man is defined first of all by his responsibility towards his brothers and towards history."[8]

The Church here associates itself with this new humanism. This sounds startling at first. How can the Christian Church identify itself with a humanism in which man is understood first of all, not in relation to God, but in relation to the human family and its history? Is this not the betrayal of the Christian

[7] Cf. Leslie Dewart, *The Future of Belief* (New York and London, 1966), pp. 64–72.

[8] Const. on the Church in the Modern World, *Lumen Gentium*, n. 55.

tradition? For the Christian who still entertains the classical form of the God question, this sentence on the new humanism must surely be a stumbling-block. But when we place this sentence and the paragraph from which it is taken into the entire conciliar document, it becomes clear that the divine is not forgotten: the divine dimension, i.e., the supernatural, is understood to be implicit in man's growing responsibility for his brothers and for history. In the perspective of contemporary theology, God is the redemptive mystery present in human life and revealed in Jesus Christ, which frees men from the bondage of the superficial and the self-centred, which enables men to discern and wrestle with the destructive powers in human life, and which opens men to the healing and elevating of life that continues to be offered to them in their history.

The question about God has become a question about God's presence in human life as creator and redeemer, i.e., the question about the meaning and destiny of history, personal and social.

The first Catholic theologian who understood the God question in the new light was Maurice Blondel, at the turn of the century.[9] While he did not pay much attention to the wider social and political aspects of man's self-making, he regarded man's personal self-making, i.e., his personal history, as the locus of the supernatural, and showed that life itself confronted men with the crucial question about the divine. In life itself every man is again and again made to choose whether to be closed, locked himself in his finite world, and cling to fixed categories for interpreting his experience, or whether to be open, let go his fixed and finite view of reality, and accept the possibility of a new consciousness, created by a mystery that transcends him. This choice, Blondel held, did not take place in man's mind but in his action, i.e., in his vital commitment and orientation. It is in life that God's gift of himself is offered to men.

Today few theologians follow Blondel's phenomenology of the human spirit. At the same time, ever since his day a growing number of theologians agree with him that the classical question about God is not the crucial question about the divine. The

---

[9] *Letter on Apologetics and History and Dogma* (London, 1964).

classical formulation "Is there a God? Does God exist?" in a sense obscures the crucial issue of human life and the Christian Gospel: it seems to imply that the question of God is posed and answered first of all in the intellect and then, once it has been settled, gives rise to a new practical relationship to life. Today many Christians hold that this is an inversion of what actually takes place in man's encounter with the divine. First, they think, is man's commitment to life: it is here that the divine mystery offers itself to him. By a response to life expressed in action and attitude, man either opens himself to a new future or locks himself into the past. Theologians describe this choice, this question-and-response, in various ways. Since the question is graciously built into life, it is no longer easy to find a definitive and unambiguous formulation of it. Some theologians focus on man's involvement in personal life, on his openness to the new, his willingness to face the dimension of evil, his conversion or breakthrough to new personal consciousness, while others concentrate more on man's involvement in social and political life, his openness to a new order, his willingness to face the dimension of evil in society, the breakthrough to a new social consciousness. In either case it is in life itself that this question about God is posed. The concept of God and the statement that he exists are produced by men's reflection on his presence in history and no one can lay hold of these unless he has affirmatively responded to the divine presence in actual life.

Klaus Schäfer

# Jesus on God

## I. The Question

WHENEVER changes in the God question are under discussion, Jesus' references to "God" have to be taken into account. When, as Christians, we want to talk about "God", we not only have to seek information from Plato, Augustine, Hegel, Feuerbach, Marx, Nietzsche, Freud and Whitehead, but have, above all, to go back to what Jesus said about "God". This is the conviction of many Christians and many theologians. Attention to Jesus' discourse about God combines study (conducted by various groups and in various forms) of the earthly Jesus of Nazareth with interest in an ultimate, inclusive, orienting and inspiriting reality: with, that is, the quest for what, in traditional religious language, is known as "God".

Jesus' talk about "God" was *"indirect"* and *"practical"*. What is intended by the use of these two terms in regard to Jesus' discourse about God, and hence in regard to the God of Jesus, should become clear in the course of this article. Jesus' parables are to the fore here, since they constitute an appropriately authentic part of the Jesus tradition, and also convey what Jesus was concerned about: the imminent kingdom of God. However, Jesus spoke in an essentially "indirect" and "practical" way about God, not only in his parables but in his "teachings" and summary statements on individual problems (for instance, on the sabbath, on marriage, on ritual purity, on fasting). What kind of reality is this that can and must be spoken of so "indirectly" and "practically"?

## II. THREE PRELIMINARY CONJECTURES

1. Jesus does not use the word "God", or other associated words and phrases, such as "kingdom of God", "eternal life" and "father", as names that allow direct linguistic representation of a reality. And he does not use such words as expressions which enable one linguistically to affirm or deny certain features as proper to an already known reality. The word *"indirect"* is intended to indicate this fact and to pose the question of how Jesus' talk about God appears, and what the fact that Jesus speaks about "God" in this particular way implies in regard to this God that is Jesus' God.

Jesus did not instruct his audience by means of theoretical pronouncements about a reality called "God". Since he had no theory about such an already known reality, he did not, therefore, wish to induce his audience to accept any such theory as correct theory. The word *"practical"* indicates this fact and poses the question of the meaning of Jesus' invocation of "God" in actual situations (healing the sick, to forgiving sins, deviant behaviour, commerce with the socially unacceptable). What kind of reality is this that is invoked in terms of a man's unforeseen behaviour in a specific situation?

2. I have put the word "God" in quotation marks up to this point in order to remove the impression of familiarity and obviousness. There are interpretations which see Jesus as a Palestinian Jew who, like everyone in his environment, believed in higher beings (God, angels, devils), but whose achievement and significance reside not in this socio-culturally conditioned religiousness, but in his teachings and exemplary life. This view does not accord with the linguistic and historical findings. Jesus' behaviour and pronouncements were condemned by the politically fashionable Jewish groups of his time as constituting an attack on the official God of the people, of the law, and of the Temple. It was Jesus' talk about "God" (for instance, his assertion that the time of joy and freedom, the time of "God", had arrived) that cost him his life. Jesus replaced the "God" of his adversaries with the reality that gave expression to his behaviour and his statements. That which his actions and his words specified, he invoked as the reality that was meaningful in itself, all-inclusive and all-determinative, final and, therefore,

ultimate in the future; that is, he understood it as "God". When
he takes away the sins of another, frequents those who are dis-
criminated against; when he shows clearly in his parables what
he thinks is timely: then something is at work which uncondi-
tionally concerns those involved and advances the word "God"
towards its true content. In Jesus' activity there is decided that
which, in terms of its "appearance", may quite justifiably be
termed "God". But what is really at issue is not this word, but
what happens. The reality which is called "God" in religious
language may be experienced as initiated by Jesus and as they
have become possible since then: in, for instance, the event of
love, which brings men together, changes them, and makes them
once more capable of life and activity.

   3. Under what heading are we to approach Jesus' talk about
God, in order to do it as much justice as possible? We can ask:
*How* did Jesus speak of God as distinct from the way of speaking
about God usual among his fellow countrymen and the two first
generations of Christians? Here we start with *stylistic* facts. We
can ask: *What* did Jesus say about God that was new in comparison to the Judaism of his time? Here we start from the basis
of the meaning of expressions typical of Jesus' usage, such as
"Abba", "kingdom of God", "enter into life"; here the question
has a *semantic* orientation. We can ask: *Where* did Jesus speak
about God? In what situations, with what kinds of people? How
were the situation and the attitude of the people concerned
changed? Here it is a question of the process between Jesus and
the people he was talking to. The style, syntax and meaning of
Jesus' words are interpreted on the basis of this "language event".
Jesus' talk about God becomes a question of *pragmatics*. Other
approaches are possible. What is the intrinsic nature of the *stories*
that Jesus told? Here attention is focused on the individual
parable as an independent, artistically organized, intrinsically (by
virtue of its components and their association) meaningful linguistic construct. Jesus' message, in this view, does not refer
primarily to something else, but is intrinsically meaningful.
Finally, it is possible to try to establish a *model* of communication and linguistic performance which does justice to these several viewpoints, and starts from the fact that Jesus' talk about God
is unified activity conditioned by several factors. Take, for in-

stance, a story like that of the "sinner" in Luke (7. 36–50): in a specific situation (constituted here by the meal, the attitude of the host and the woman's behaviour), Jesus addresses himself to the person who needs his word (in this case, the host). By means of a story he shows him what is happening at the moment: a man is thankful that he can start afresh. The process has six factors: the transmitter (Jesus), the receiver (Simon), the common linguistic system (it determines Jesus' story), the common situation (the given circumstances, the people concerned, their behaviour), a communication medium (the spoken word, sound), and finally the communication itself (the story of the two debtors, Luke 7. 41–3). In accordance with the six factors involved, six possible linguistic achievements are to be distinguished. The speaker can express himself. The receiver can be influenced. The situation (the "context") can be represented. The communication process can be controlled. The system of common understanding can be linguistically explicated as such. Attention can be given to the text as such. In this view, it is the decisive linguistic act; its form, its meaning, its import and itself as an aesthetic phenomenon.

## III. Three Further Viewpoints

The foregoing model of the factors and products of linguistic communication can help to advance our understanding of Jesus' discourse about God. Anyone who tries to examine Jesus' indirect and practical talk about God by means of this model, would have, for example (from the viewpoint of the transmission medium), to explain how Jesus' deviant behaviour required him to comment verbally on this sign-action, and how, on the other hand, a situation is brought out and clarified by Jesus' word (e.g., Luke 15. 1, 2 or Mark 2. 5; 2. 3). He would have to show how Jesus' talk about God is *performative*, a mode of behaviour. From the viewpoint of the receiver, it would have to be shown how Jesus approaches the interests and possibilities of understanding of his audience in order to transform them into the something new that he presents in his narrative, and how at the same time he provokes to protest in order to make conscious the conflict between himself and them. He would also have to show how Jesus brings his audience closer to a new understanding of their existence—which also opens their eyes to the neighbour they had until then despised or neglected (e.g., Matt. 20. 1–16 or Luke 7. 36–50). Jesus' talk about God should be interpreted as an attempt to open his audience's eyes to what has to be done now, to what is now self-obvious (e.g., Luke 15. 11–32). In the "context" aspect, consideration would have to be given, e.g., to the extent to which Jesus uses plants, animals, the earth and life processes indirectly and in regard to practice in order to speak about "God" (e.g., Matt. 6. 26–28 f.; Mark 4. 26–9, 30–2). But, above all, our explicator would have to show that Jesus talks about "God" by implicitly analysing the social construction of reality, and hence the ideological bases of the "context" itself (e.g., Mark 2. 17–21 f.–27; 3. 33–5; 7. 14 f.; 10. 9; 11. 15–17; Luke 18. 9–14). For Jesus, talking about "God" means representing a future time as already effective now—a future in which the present false conditions of domination will be overcome wholly, that is by the destruction of their religio-political justification. Therefore there is indirect and practical talk about "God" wherever Jesus rescues men from a false consciousness—a socially dominative condition of anxiety and blindness. In Jesus' case, "God" is spoken of in order to draw attention to a change in domination that will alter the situation. This transition, which transforms the "context", this subversion of the dominant circumstances, also defines the "transmitter", and hence the function of Jesus himself. Jesus speaks without any official authorization from God and without any dependence on education.

For his deviant behaviour, for what is timely, he invokes the whole of, and ultimate, reality: he believes that he accords with that reality. Hence, in trying to communicate his behaviour, he opens eyes to the reality which determines the situation and intends to be understood in this its liberating power: he opens eyes to "God". By speaking indirectly of his own situation-supportive practice, Jesus makes it possible for his audience to perceive this situation as the coming of God (Luke 15. 1–7, 8–10; Matt. 13. 44–6, 47–50): it is God who here gathers men together and allows himself to be found by them. In accordance with this function, Jesus distinguishes himself from God by referring himself to him in prayer (e.g., Mark 1. 35).

A detailed account of everything that might be said under

the six viewpoints of my linguistic model in regard to my two keywords is impossible in the present article. Therefore the following remarks are restricted to an account of the two aspects of Jesus' discourse not yet referred to: language and texts.

1. To what extent is Jesus' talk about God indirect and practical in language, in its "code"?

(a) Jesus uses conventional circumlocutions when congratulating those for whom God is near at hand (e.g., Matt. 5. 9). The code of religious language is used in order to assert that the future belongs to the martyrs (Luke 6. 20b–23, 24–6). Occasionally Jesus comes near to directly religious statement. Even then he does not teach about a distant God, but invites his audience to accord in their behaviour with the nearness of God, his obligingness (e.g., Matt. 5. 44 f., 48 and Mark 10. 18).

(b) Jesus invokes a religio-political catchphrase with many associated memories and hopes: the "kingdom of God" is at hand. Men learn to forgive one another, to rejoice with one another, to overcome the shadows of their present anxieties and prejudices, to think well of one another, and to leave their social roles. These inconspicuous changes reveal a change in the conditions of domination (Mark 1. 15a, Matt. 11. 5 ff.), which Jesus' parables represent poetically. Jesus introduces profane stories into the context of his practice, which liberates men and disenchants institutions; locates the old phrase "kingdom of God" in this non-religious linguistic field; and in this "code" brings the word "God" into play once again. Hence religious words are introduced into a *practical* context of action, so that *indirectly* they qualify this new practice as the only one with the future before it (Luke 11. 20 and 17. 21).

(c) Jesus uses the word "Abba" to address the reality that has determined him. This children's word was used by those who knew one another and understood one another, who belonged and worked together. Jesus can talk to God as a human being and address him as "Father", because he sees that God's closeness makes men happy (Luke 10. 21–4; Mark 2. 13–7). When he speaks out of this experience to assert that something good is happening about him, and speaks to others about God as the "Father", then he is inviting them to be touched by his joy in God and to entrust themselves to what is now happening, since

the future belongs to this Good (Mark 10. 27; Matt. 7. 7–11).
Here again, Jesus' discourse is indirect and practical.

2. To what extent does Jesus speak practically and indirectly
of God in his "texts"?

(*a*) Jesus tells stories. He always describes common processes
from domestic and agricultural life. He "quotes" interesting
special cases from the areas of social, economic and family life.
He invents people and events and uses them as examples. Everything takes place in the world in which Jesus and his audience
live. What is described can happen at any time: at least as an exception. Jesus narrates in the same way as the man in the street
offers judgment: straightforwardly, briefly, with suspense, but
without sentimentality, focusing on the protagonists and their
actions. He emphasizes dialogue scenes, occasions of recognition
and of decision about happiness or unhappiness. The conflicts
usually have some socio-economic determination. It is a matter
of debts, wages, taxes, tenancies, of social and economic ups and
downs, and of physical existence. Normal men play socially
normal roles: father and son, masters and servants, creditors and
debtors, employers and employees, the better people and those
from the other side of the tracks. They are described in terms of
their attitudes and their realistic or foolish behaviour. In these
stories God is spoken about only indirectly, in the framework
and implications of the action, in the attitudes and interactions
of the participants.

(*b*) In several respects, there is no talk of God. Neither he nor
other higher beings enter in. The scenery usually has nothing to
do with religion (Luke 18. 9–14 is the exception). Ministers of
religion occur only once—as an example to show that religion
can lead to reality being ignored (Luke 10. 31 f.). The material
of conflict and the processes that decide conflict are usually non-
religious. Wherever the reality of God occurs in a story, the
word "God" is avoided: because God is beginning to rule, inasmuch as men are coming closer to one another, there is no need
to talk about him (Luke 10. 33–5). But God is also not placed—
in the style of allegory—"behind" specific individuals. The father
(1 Luke 15. 11–32) and the owner of the vineyard (Matt. 20. 1–16)
do not stand for a higher being in their attitude and behaviour
but are to be understood in terms of their attitude, behaviour and

place in the story. The goodness of these and many other of the actors in Jesus' stories is improbable, not predictable. It suddenly breaks out. Since the stories are wholly determined by this sudden appearance of paradoxical goodness, they show what is now at hand. The time of goodness has arrived. Whoever welcomes this time accords with reality: with, that is, God.

(c) Jesus' parables talk indirectly and practically about God by showing what is now at hand and where God is to be found. It is time to rejoice, because God is to be found (Matt. 13. 44–6). It is time to decide whether to live with others and to bear with one another, or to live instead for oneself (Matt. 13. 47 f., 24–30). From now on people can rest assured that time is working for God (Mark 4. 26–9), since already that insignificant beginning which Jesus has made, makes the future certain (Mark 4. 30–2).

But this time, now available, is to be made use of (Luke 16. 1–7), for God awaits us where men need us (Luke 10. 30–5). Jesus speaks indirectly and practically of God by referring us to those who without (or because of?) us would remain on the roadside.

*Works referred to in writing this article*

G. Bornkamm, *Jesus von Nazareth* (Stuttgart, 1959).

H. Braun, *Jesus* (Stuttgart, 1969).

R. Bultmann, *Die Geschichte der synoptischen Tradition* (Göttingen, 1961).

G. Eichholz, *Gleichnisse der Evangelien* (Neukirchen-Vluyn, 1971).

E. Fuchs, *Zur Frage nach dem historischen Jesus* (Tübingen, 1960).

E. Fuchs, *Jesus Wort und Tat* (Tübingen, 1971).

E. Güttgemanns, *Studia linguistica neotestamenica* (Munich, 1971).

E. Haenchen, *Der Weg Jesu* (Berlin, 1966).

J. Jeremias, *Die Gleichnisse Jesus* (Göttingen, 1956).

J. Jeremias, *Neutestamentliche Theologie*, Part 1 (Gütersloh, 1971).

E. Jüngel, *Paulus und Jesus* (Tübingen, 1964).

F. Kambartel, "Teo-Logisches", *Zeitschr. f. ev. Ethik*, 15 (1971), pp. 32–5.

L. Kolakowski, *Geist und Ungeist christlicher Traditionen* (Stuttgart, 1971).

W. G. Kümmel, *Die Theologie des Neuen Testaments nach seinen Hauptzeugen: Jesus, Paulus, Johannes* (Göttingen, 1969).

E. Linnemann, *Gleichnisse Jesus* (Göttingen, 1962).

K. Niederwimmer, *Jesus* (Göttingen, 1968).

W. Pannenberg, *Theologie und Reich Gottes* (Gütersloh, 1971).

R. Schäfer, *Jesus und der Gottesglaube* (Tübingen, 1970).

H. Schürmann, *Traditionsgeschichtliche Untersuchungen zu den synoptischen Evangelien* (Düsseldorf, 1968).

D. Sölle, *Das Recht ein anderer zu werden* (Neuwied & Berlin, 1971).

D. O. Via, *Die Gleichnisse Jesus* (Munich, 1970).

H. Zimmermann, *Neutestamentliche Methodenlehre* (Stuttgart, 1967).

*Translated by John Griffiths*

Alain Durand

# Political Implications
# of the God Question

is increasing attention paid to the political implications of the God
question because of its actual content, or because we no longer
know how to pose the very question of God? Is it because a large
number of people are no longer interested in God that we try,
without any real assurance, to refurbish the old image a little by
borrowing the lustre that attaches nowadays to a "political" treatment of any question? Is this part of the search for truth or just
a piece of religious opportunism?

It is obviously possible to argue, since we no longer have any
specific language for talking about God himself, that we have to
resort (according to the opportunities offered by time and place)
to the languages proper to metaphysics, cosmology, psychology,
literary criticism or politics. Hence theology may talk meta-
physically, psychologically or politically about God for the simple
reason that it cannot talk about him "divinely"; yet this does not
mean that theology is trying in any way to elevate any one of
these languages (from an absolute viewpoint) above God himself.

Is the cultural context the only (pragmatic) justification for the
mode of discourse chosen by the theologian? If God revealed himself in a specific place and at a specific time, we are referred to a
normative choice which excludes talk about God on the basis of
just any reality in our cultural field. To deny this would be equivalent to identifying God's revelation with the totality of the world,
and therefore to deny the actual history of God's revelation.

Does this mean that it is fidelity to the authentic countenance
of God revealed in Jesus Christ that makes us ask if the God

question is political? Or is it simply that we are reaching desperately for our last possible justification in this matter?

## I. THE GOD QUESTION HAS A POLITICAL HISTORY

First of all we have to take a quite irrefutable fact into account: the God question is very much a political matter in the perspective of our own history. Until very recently, religious life was an inalienable dimension of the political community. To believe in God was not something superfluous which political society could have dispensed with. On the contrary, everything would seem to indicate that the religious bond was indispensable for the very existence of a social bond. Bacon said that religion was the main social bond. Religious beliefs were not a matter for the individual conscience alone: they constituted a political problem inasmuch as a society enjoyed cohesion by virtue of a collective and institutionalized identification of the world of the gods. Heresy became a political crime just as the political opposition assumed a religious expression. At the beginning of our era, Christianity came into conflict with ancient Rome as a religious and not as a political movement. But this religious force was a political threat in that it developed because the unity of Europe and the power of the Emperor laid claim to a religious basis. The question of God became a political problem by reason of the type of society in question. When the pagan religion was no longer able to ensure this political unity, another religion seemed, because of its success, apt to fulfil the same role: thus the God of Jesus Christ succeeded the gods of the Pantheon. Before bewailing this politically compromising aspect of the Constantinian Church, we must try to understand it by the logic of such a society. The question of God is a political question if only because a (political) society lays claim to a religious basis.

Today, in some of our societies at least, that situation no longer applies: religion has become a "private matter" in the sense that membership of political society no longer has an aspect of collective and institutionalized religious identification.[1] There was a

[1] The following pages do not pretend throughout to a universal truth of reference. They were written for the most part (though not exclusively) with French society in mind. On the other hand, a number of details might well be added to the text in regard to the emancipation of politics

major break. A social order no longer refers to a repertoire of specific religious beliefs. The social bond is made and an overall consensus operates outside the religious universe. Religion is no longer the integrating element in our societies, even though at the level of consciousness of some individuals and groups religious convictions still constitute a powerful integrative (or separative) factor. Inasmuch as these groups exist, the world of their religious representations could eventually come into play as a support for the established society, or for oppositional forces present in that society—but this is *primarily* the problem of these groups, and not of society as a whole. The question of God has become marginal politically, now that the main organizational axis of political society is no longer religious.

Nevertheless, however marginal and superficial it may seem, the God question (where it does exist) is not politically neutral. It possesses its political implications not, now, by reason of the religious nature of political society, but because of the autonomy and universality that have accrued to political society itself. In order to understand what this means, a brief characterization of this society is necessary.

## II. What is Political Society?

The term "political" necessarily refers to a social whole structured by means of institutions or, if preferred, to institutions which structure men in a given whole. In the strict sense, society itself is the political reality. An action is political to the extent that, directly or indirectly, in the short or the long term, it contributes to the maintenance of the present structure of that whole, or to its modification in order to produce a differently structured totality. Because of certain changes (among which industrialization is of major importance), interdependence between the different members of the political community has increased, become more diversified, and been considerably modified to the point of giving rise to new classes. A certain number of processes have themselves become increasingly universal, and more co-extensive

---

in relation to religion, and the analysis of the political superdetermination of religious issues. Obviously space is insufficient for discussion of such finer points.

with political society. Hence economic life is no longer a matter
of small human units isolated from one another within the
larger whole constituted by the political community. Its universality extends throughout this very whole. On the level of production, of distribution or of consumption, the structures of
economic life are now global structures of our society. In this
sense, economy today has become political reality.

But the different levels or contents of human existence are also
increasingly dependent on these overall structures. The family,
which has been gradually reduced from a functional whole, is
especially significant in this respect, for its functions have now
devolved upon larger institutions (economic production, leisure,
health and geriatric services). The destiny of family life nowadays is played out largely within the family itself. Other examples
are possible. The originality of our situation resides perhaps in
the fact that control of a particular area depends increasingly on
control of the whole.

Of course, one should not overemphasize the situation. There
are, on the one hand, processes which accord increasingly in universality with the dimensions of political society (or even extend
beyond its territorial bounds), and, on the other hand, the diverse
issues of human life depend more and more on these universalized
processes. The whole of human existence is *informed* (in the strict
sense of the word) through and through by political reality.
Not everything is political; in the sense, that is, that there are
other questions in human life than those which have to do with
the general organization of human relations and with the interaction of the forces producing this organization. Yet everything
is political in the sense that nothing exists without first of all
being conditioned by this organization and, then, without exert-
ing a positive or negative influence on it. The religious phenomenon, considered in terms of beliefs, dogmas, rites and the
various institutionalizations which it produces, does not escape
this general law.


III. Present Political Treatment of the God Question.
Ideology, Politics and Theology

We can now try to understand in greater detail the present

political implications of the God question, and to see under what conditions a politically aware theological discussion could include talk about God.

1. Inasmuch as political society does not rely on a collective and socialized religious foundation: to the extent, that is, that it possesses a specific autonomy in relation to religious questions, it also possesses more actual universality than they do. The religious phenomenon is therefore one of the multifarious internal determinations produced within a reality more inclusive than itself: the reality of political society. In contradistinction to what could occur in the previous situation, henceforth religions can enjoy a certain degree of "free play" which does not affect the organization of political society as directly as in the past. This is the return for the loss of universality. It is also what is known as the "age of tolerance".

2. Inasmuch as political society is the only inclusive reality, it is also the basis of a political superdetermination of religious questions. The emancipation of politics in relation to religion does not imply a symmetrical emancipation of religion in relation to politics. Autonomy is not absolutely reciprocal. Religious questions are open to free debate without political society feeling itself *ipso facto* concerned, since (on the one hand) it no longer lays claim to a religious foundation, and (on the other) religious questions no longer enjoy a universality coextensive with that of political society. It is precisely because this "free play" enjoyed by religious questions is situated within political society that it is superdetermined by the latter. But, in order to comprehend how religious questions are superdetermined by the actual universality of political society, we must remember that this universality is not neutral. The present structure of political society is not simply to be equated with service to all its citizens. It gives privileged service to the private interests of certain groups or classes. In addition, the same classes, as long as there is no critical political awareness among the dominated, exercise an ideological ascendancy over the whole of society, to the extent that the dominant ideology is one and the same as the ideology of the dominant classes. Under these conditions, the political superdetermination of religious questions operates spontaneously. It is part of the very logic of such a society that the God question should be treated in

the manner most favourable to the interests of the dominant classes: that is, of the classes which profit from the actual universality of political society. We must be aware of this. The case cannot very well be otherwise so long as there is no critical and political consciousness among those studying the question of God.

3. The foregoing account is supported by the way in which the Church has treated religious questions in its recent past. The very question of God has been politicized in regard to the type of universality predominant in a society transformed by the birth of capitalism. The Church became structurally marginal in modern society, and looked for new means of integration. The influence of the "partial" universality of political society was all the stronger inasmuch as the Church faced up to its own marginalization by retaining its nostalgia for the dominant position it occupied in medieval society. Once marginalized, it had to find a new "social excuse" that would allow it justification in the eyes of society. The Church proved its usefulness in putting its charitable resources at the disposal of existing society, and offering religious remedies in order to make the misfortunes of the age more bearable. Within this society it found gaps which allowed it to make itself useful: interim functions which gave it a way in. Some Catholics even declared that the State should not care for the poor, since that was a function God had reserved for his Church. In doing this the Church remained wholly within the limits of established society and respect for the powers that be. This God who has created rich and poor, while taking a mite more alms from the first and offering the second the consolations of the after-life (God as he appeared in *Rerum Novarum*, for example), had the ideological features of the bourgeoisie. Trying to justify its existence on the basis of society as it was (just as today there is an attempt to seek God "on the basis of life"—but which life?), the Church simultaneously prevented itself from debating that society. Its will to integration (it does not really matter whether this was conscious or unconscious) prevented it from justifying its existence on the basis of a future which it might have helped to provoke in place of the *status quo*. The passage from a "social Christianity" to a "political Christianity" would surely be the sign of an abandonment of this process of integration, of a growing emancipation from ideology and dominant

powers, and would surely coincide with the birth of a really political investigation of the very structures of our society.

4. It would be naïve to imagine that the image of a God who created some rich and others poor, and who asks them all to collaborate in brotherhood was invented to serve capitalist society! It existed before capitalism. But the same image acquired a new political significance because of the new context. In an age in which men realize that they have real power over the very structures of their social existence, to maintain such an image of God is to oppose any movement that might try to exert that power. That the Church preaches such an image of God in a society where the historical possibilities for change are minimal is hardly of consequence. But it is politically serious in another type of society. By the specific way in which it presents God, the Church takes up a certain political position.

5. The political superdetermination of religious questions does not mean that specific modifications cannot be produced in the "private" field of religious beliefs, or that such modifications are without political consequence. In fact, a change in the image of God can be dysfunctional in relation to the actual organization of political society, inasmuch as that organization is consolidated by the religious legitimation some people can give it. This evidently means that such believers represent a significant political force in the society in question, and that there is an effective relation—variously mediated—between the image they have of God and the means by which they determine themselves politically (or believe they do not determine themselves). A change in religious images can lose the social organization a far from negligible support. The God question can even comprise so obvious a political issue that some people quite readily take part in religious debates for strictly political ends. In France, for example, the Academician M. Druon, while declaring himself drawn more to Epictetus than to Jesus Christ, nevertheless supports a return to the "sacred" in the Church, because he knows that the new situation will not help the political stability of the kind of society he likes.[2] Conversely, a Marxist like Casanova is very interested in the changes in the God image of Catholics, since he knows that

[2] M. Druon, "Une Eglise qui se trompe de siècle", *Le Monde* (7 August 1971).

this is one of the elements he has to take into account among those that could contribute to a changed society.[3] Though it has lost the central position once accorded it officially, the God question is no less political.

\*           \*           \*

The God question is subject to the influence of the dominant universal political mode so long as those interested in it are not critically aware of their political situation. Until we reach such a growth of awareness, there is, I think, room for a theology of witness to the situation, or for a messianic theology, but not for a politically aware theology. Before an increase of political awareness, religious questions must be subject to the tendency imposed by the partial universality of political society, or must oppose it by taking messianic and therefore pre-political forms. It is not enough to argue from revelation in order to emancipate the God question from the dominant ideology. This is, admittedly, one of the necessary aspects of the theological quest, but it is difficult to see how it could help this discourse to escape the hold of the actual organization of political society. Theological discourse can escape serving the dominant classes only by criticism of their ideology.

Participation in such a critique does not mean that theological discourse must then submit directly to an opposed ideology. If that were the case, it would cease to be critical. But, in mankind's present situation, liberty is a possibility only if there is recourse *initially* to criticism of the ideology of the ruling classes and, *afterwards*, constant vigilance in regard to all ideological production—which is something quite different to a neutralist stance. Even though faith is not an ideology, there is no faith without ideology, any more than there is a God question without political implications. It is well to be aware of this.

Since the deficiency from which we suffer is the result mainly of a lack of critical political awareness, only an incursion of critical consciousness into theology will free the God question from the supposed political innocence in which some people hope to preserve it.

*Translated by John Griffiths*

[3] A. Casanova, *Vatican II et l'évolution de l'Eglise* (Paris, 1969).

# André Dumas

# God as Protest against the "Death of Man"

THE God concept is no longer operative in contemporary thought. I use the word "concept" in order to emphasize from the start that God himself, the non-conceptualizable living God, is not in his actuality dependent on the functions that our knowledge allows him. If he is God, he is not created by the apprehensions of our intellects. That which is proper to God, in contradistinction to the divine, is not to be the attribute that we confer upon the ultimate dimension of our human experience, but to confront this experience as an otherness that this experience could not conceive.

God is neither the extension nor the peak of the human, but that which lies over against it and allows of incarnation as distinct from infusion. The biblical notion of God insists firmly on this element of otherness: of power over against that proper to man, in the sense that to have God as an "adversary" is full of promise for man, if man can convert God into a partner, since for man everything depends on the will of God. As Gottfried Quell writes: "He is the power with which man cannot compete.... Very probably, the notion of power was the fundamental concept in the Semitic understanding of the divine being."[1] In Greek thought, however, the divine was man's expression of his perception of the harmonious coherence of the whole cosmos, and represented a gradual movement beyond our restricted

[1] Gottfried Quell, "El et Elohim dans l'Ancien Testament", article "theos" in *Theologisches Wörterbuch zum Neuem Testament* (Stuttgart, 1938), Vol. 3, p. 84.

and too anthropomorphic intuitions of the world. "The history of thought in classical antiquity reveals ... a conception of God as an essence which guarantees stability."[2] On the one hand, God is a sovereign force in no way dependent on our perception, conception or imagination, since we instead depend on his decision to reveal or hide himself; on the other hand, the divine is that which is accomplished and perceived by man at the most refined heights of speculation.

One might reject (as insignificant in terms of God's reality) the loss of function of the God concept in human intellectual discourse, and even maintain that the present lack of philosophic viability of the divine was the best situation in which to rediscover that the intervention of God is something quite other than the human elaboration of that same divine something. As a contemporary philosopher, Gérard Granel, is justified in asserting: "There is no problem for God.... There is some kind of obscure belief that nowadays God must, so to speak, be (in some special way) grappling with his own difficulty, contrary to his transcendence and his absolute otherness for man. But if the matter is seen from God's viewpoint, clearly he (himself) has always managed very well indeed as far as this supposed dilemma is concerned; the characteristics of our age are certainly not more apt than those of any other to form a barrier for the Almighty."[3]

Nowadays hermeneutics is so inflated at the expense of dogmatic theology that there is a risk of the ludicrous assumption that the human intellect is the ground of God's reality; that man is a condition for God, and God the divine product of our own procedure. Such an assertion would confuse (on behalf of the crisis situation of the concept of the divine in contemporary philosophy) negative ontology with the same theology that is henceforth declared impossible. If man no longer poses the question of the divine, he declares that God can no longer assert himself as a personal other. Then we block the transcendence of God in the midst of the difficulties experienced by human immanence in its attempts to derive, finalize or totalize itself. We transfer to

[2] Hermann Kleinknecht, "La notion grecque de Dieu", *Theologisches Wörterbuch zum Neuem Testament, op. cit.,* p. 78.
[3] Gérard Granel, "Sur la situation de l'incroyance", *Esprit,* January 1971, p. 4.

God the embarrassments of the human view of the divine. This is a logically senseless and theologically confused argument which supposes that our conditions of possibility presuppose a reality which, in terms of its own legality, does not depend on them.

## I. ORGANIZED SOCIETY AND SOCIAL PRACTICE

On both sides of the Atlantic we have experienced in recent years a reduction of what since the Renaissance has gone by the name of "humanism": of, that is, the affirmation of the transcendence of their environment by human reflective thought and human action. That glorious (or at least elevated) pedestal man allowed himself as the sole location of the world in terms of freedom, has been upset. Man now occupies a more modest position—one decided more by other factors and, perhaps, more insignificant, among all that is. In order to try to understand this reduction of humanist transcendentalism, I shall allude briefly to the technological development of modern society, stressing above all the most recent emphases, without claiming however that the infrastructure of the first determines the superstructures of the second—which is, nevertheless, a polemical argument against present developments, and one used by those very commentators who (in regard to this particular situation) had always rejected the theory of a dependent consciousness.

A major characteristic of our society is the extension of memory by means of machines. The first industrial revolution relieved mankind of muscular effort, by liberating the latent energy contained in matter and making it available for man's projects. The second industrial revolution relieved mankind of mental effort, by building machines to calculate, programme, store, sort and resolve with infinitely greater speed, regularity and range than men ever could. We call such machines "intelligent" because they work with elements characteristic of intelligence, if the latter is distinguished from intuition, demonstration and imagination, as the faculty of ordering, synthesizing and discovering the most economical consequence for a complex situation. These new machines are also able to react to new elements which are fed to them or which they encounter in the course of operation. These they integrate and correct automatically by means of a control system that allows them constantly to adapt to transformations. These machines can absorb an astonishing quantity of facts and maintain appropriate equilibrium on encountering the new elements they register, and are able simultaneously to eliminate any too heterogeneous contributions in order to ensure integration in the agreed system, and by means of a series of retroactions and anticipations to retain the initial programme. These machines possess the three characteristics Jean Piaget has attributed to structures: formalization of a totality, relational transformations, and selective self-regulation.[4] Of course there is nothing surprising in the fact that the term "system" (usually reserved for human cerebral activity) tends to be generalized and applied to anything featuring elements of regularity, and interactions within a whole so closed as to constitute an effective relational field.

Everything here is directed towards decreased surprise and increased integration; towards the suppression of liberty, considered as an as yet unprogrammed danger, in favour of necessity, understood as lucid rationality. A certain model of knowledge predominates—one assuring optimal clarity in exchange processes, and maximal rigour in operations, without any more insoluble questions as to the origin, end, and even the content and meaning of what is at stake. The supreme value here is not spontaneity (which is a subjective remnant of a prescientific mentality), but organization as the expression of the deepest tendency of mind (and perhaps of the world) to become a coherence in contradistinction to chaos, and to order itself instead of exploding and dispersing. As Witold Gombrowicz writes: "Form is never appropriate to essence. Nevertheless any thought which tries to define the nature of this inappropriateness of form in its turn becomes form and thus confirms our tendency towards form."[5]

There is no doubt that our society participates to a large extent in this sociology of knowledge; the "small extent" being the extreme opposite of this ideology of organization: revolution as permanent revolt and as the utopia of the not-possible. The latest thing in society is not productivity (which no longer fascinates

[4] Jean Piaget, *Structuralism* (New York & London, 1971), Chapter 1.
[5] Cited as the epigraph to Jean Ehrmann's *Structuralism* (New York, 1970).

the human spirit), but the provisional nature of the projects undertaken. Once it is admitted that one is operating within a framework of a certain number of facts (whether it is a question of linguistic, ethnological, economic or political suasions), one may (at first) assert that the number of possible combinations is not infinite, but that the most rational solution (also the most lucid logically, most attractive aesthetically, and least expensive economically) is unique in each situation. This would mean that society would no longer be an ideological, arbitrary and confused melting-pot, but become a theoretical, scientifically experimenting system. This was the dream of positivism: to eliminate the theological and metaphysical perspectives which everyone could debate about for ever without arriving at a universally demonstrable scientific explanation. Yet now positivism, after the romanticism of existentialism and the first, voluntarist and utopian, versions of Marxism, would seem to have been reborn.

There are, however, two seemingly original features of what, in the mid-twentieth century, is known vaguely as "structuralism", as distinct from the positivism of the mid-nineteenth century. First of all, the notion of positivism is radically eliminated inasmuch as the tendency to form—to organization—is acknowledged by ethnologists to have been present in all human societies that have ever existed. Researchers have totally rejected any right to classify as prelogical the mentalities of societies without history and without science, that is, history as a totalizing chronology and science as a mechanical causality. Instead, modern man and modern society are deluded into believing it possible to give birth to a totally new world, when all they do is to potter with the old world, which remains identical throughout its various systems of organization. A comparativist and relativistic wisdom has replaced a progressivist and absolutist self-assertion.

Auguste Comte, who like Karl Marx was heir to the philosophy of the eighteenth-century Enlightenment, believed that the third phase of positivism would surpass the preceding stages, and that humanity would advance towards an unclouded heaven under the aegis of scientific knowledge. There is no trace of this evolutionist optimism in contemporary thinkers. Having renounced the idea of a total history, and remaining content with local epistemologies, they are often closer to Nietzsche and to his acknowledgment of the eternal return, than to Marx and his expectation of the new man, even though the latter is more scientific than messianic or utopian. The neo-Positivists do not agree that the regularity of scientific causalities is more rational than that of mythic mediations, since in both cases rules structure and order social practice in a like manner. There is no longer any question of a Bergsonian opposition to open societies; instead the attraction is exerted (through heroic example and mystic revelation) by closed societies still very near to animal instincts, for it is the notion of closedness which properly constitutes any society both as a co-ordinated whole and as an object for investigation. Still less is there any question, as with Sartre, of exalting the moment of free and unanimous fusion, the fervent instant of revolt, at the expense of the contiguity of the inert sequence which preceded it, and of the institutional repetition which follows it, since—properly—the categories of sequence and repetition are those which ground any practicable and observable human society. Progress is therefore a subjective pretension which objective knowledge ought to learn to do without. By this rejection modern man reacquires that equal brotherhood with all preceding generations, which—like us—were concerned to bring about that reconciliation of irreconciliables that is the warp and woof of the world. There is no better way to see the modification brought about by this new perspective than reflection on the new meaning of the word "dialectic" in the light of the foregoing. Whereas in those philosophies which depend on progress (whether they be individual or collective) dialectics aims at the orientation of procedure by an ascending axis, perhaps in association with a synthetic vision or realization, in the new version "dialectic" denotes the study of horizontal mediations between permanently opposed poles. There is no longer any question of an advance into history but a quest for mediation in a field of experience and knowledge. The notion of synthesis disappears totally; for if it were ever to come about, synthesis would destroy the goal of human activity, which is unceasingly to relate opposed data. Whereas the structure postulated by the philosophers of progress was more or less trinitarian, with totalization in progress, the structure of the new form of knowledge is resolutely binary, since structuralist analysis is interested not in the totalization of rela-

tions, but in relations themselves. This alone is a sufficient indica-
tion of how modern neo-Positivism differs from the previous
form.

A second point is just as important. Most relations in the structures under investigation are experienced unconsciously by those
who "practise" them. It is a question of hidden relations, whose
deep laws the social scientist is often more adequately equipped
to reconstruct than those originally and actively concerned. Obviously psychoanalysis has strongly influenced such a view of
society. Knowledge would, in this view, consist less in provoking
consciousness to initiate history than in deciphering the hidden
mechanisms of composition, which, behind the apparent in-
coherence of the overly reconstructed coherence, in reality re-
establish equilibrium between opposing impulses. Much more
than in the older positivism, which was content to dissipate
mythic obscurity and metaphysical dissociation by means of the
clear light of science, we are faced here with an interpretation of
the all too apparent. What we believe to be an innovation is only
a reaction determined by a problem whose fundamental data
have been obscured by various ideologies. The work of knowledge is to rebuild the subterranean tunnels between various more
or less ruined monuments, when people are unable to see them
other than in terms of their façades and the distribution of their
visible components. It is necessary to reconstruct the concealed
structures which make every society a whole tending to organization, whatever individuals may be doing on stage while in the
wings determinative forces direct the course of things. As in any
interpretation, one is confronted finally with a set of mirrors,
where nothing is ultimate, first, or last, but everything is relational, subtly referred to another term of the problem, whose
links with the most visible term one had not initially noticed.
In this way an immense syntax is constituted, which reveals
society as a machine absorbing a mass of information, evolving
in accordance with diverse inner transformations, and incessantly
trying to integrate the new without banishing the old. Only in
this way can society become the object of scientific investigation,
as the older positivism required, but without taking into account
the fact that progressive organization had no metaphysical value
on the level of values and without seeing that the springs of

human reality are hidden, or—to put it briefly—that what characterizes man as distinct from things is less his possession of a consciousness tending towards organization than his possession of an unconscious tending to conceal true motivations.

At present there is a concurrent development of a technology of machines with memories and an ideology of organizational knowledge. I cannot establish a cause-effect relationship between these two factors, because it is far too easy to separate consciousness from socio-economic conditioning when one wants to make a protest on behalf of liberty, only to resume the argument immediately afterwards in order to refute some unwelcome consideration. We must keep to the concomitance of a technology of computers and an ideology of social regularities, if we are to avoid the contested term "structuralism".[6]

But doesn't this co-existence signify the "death of man"? This journalistic term was used first by the supporters of social regularity, before being taken up by the opponents of structuralism, almost exactly when the theologians were concerning themselves with the death of God. I find the expression misleading, whether used to assert an end to the transcendence of the human *cognito* or to deplore the loss of a humanistic freedom. In fact it is much more a question of another definition of man, no longer in terms of pre-reflexive spontaneity and creative revolt, as with Sartre, but in terms of logical regularity and interactions. Man is no longer, as in all forms of existentialism, the one who projects himself in contradistinction to the massive world of things, the one by whom the unforeseeable comes into being, the one who never coincides with himself. Man is the one who carries out transactions: mediations between things according to rules both instituted and observed. Man no longer realizes or tries to realize the indefinite history of his freedom. Man constructs an architectural whole. He incessantly tries to delimit, in order to understand and to act. Michel Foucault expresses this change of perspective in the "archaeology of knowledge" when he says that

[6] Lévi-Strauss and Althusser retain it, whereas Foucault rejects it. Piaget is reluctant to apply it straightforwardly to the human sciences, if it is not completed by "constructivism". In fact there is no School, but a convergence of methods among researchers each of whom is an expert in his own area.

henceforth it is necessary to pass from documents to monuments, from history to archaeology:[7] from, that is, a content enlivened and perceived by a conscious mind to a fixed and described organization, without asking any more questions about the conscious mind which conceived or experienced it.

If there is death here, it is the death of man as creative subjectivity for the benefit of another man, product, architect and witness of organizational objectivities which put order into things. Michel Foucault announces the disappearance of the "soft, dumb and intimate" consciousness, and its replacement by an "obscure collection of anonymous rules".[8] There is no longer any assertion of a new man or of a transformed society. There is the study of the *bricoleur*—the "do-it-yourself man" who devotes himself to the precision of his tinkerings in a universe without metaphysical transcendence, without any philosophy of history, without creative subjectivity, and—if you wish—without theology, without Hegelian Marxism, and without Sartrian Kierkegaardism.

## II. From God as Ground to God as Contingency

We may well ask after the function of the God concept in this kind of contemporary thought, which imagines it has made him more useless than any previous philosophy; for it not only continues to refute all metaphysical grounds, but suppresses the two major refuges of the God concept afforded in modern times by the sense of history and the appeal to subjectivity. Here God is rejected as the substratum of being, as historico-eschatological totalization, and as the image of existence, incessantly challenged to the point of risk, decision and faith. Here there is no hidden presence of God manifested in his visible absence, because there is a rejection of everything that was customarily connected with the word "God": essence and everlastingness, origin and end, existence and vocation, meaning and interpretation. Those who prophesied that the death of man would soon follow upon the

---

[7] The word is used in its least metaphysical sense. It is not a question of looking for an origin, but of renouncing this vain quest in order to reconstruct traces which will not be the signs of a truth located behind the traces.

[8] Michel Foucault, *L'archéologie du savoir* (Paris, 1969), p. 273.

death of God probably wished to say that it was impossible to retain for the benefit of man the major attributes traditionally
acknowledged as belonging to God. This, for example, was in
Sartre's mind when he reproached Descartes for not saying of
man exactly what he affirmed of God: that he was the free originator of values, the only justifier (in no other way justified) of the
world, and that he should courageously assert himself as the only
responsible creator of the entire universe. If there is no longer
any transcendence of God, this does not mean there will be a free
transcendence of man. Deep down, humanism will remain an
unseasonable theological relic. Anti-humanism, for which atheism
has always reproached theology, would on the contrary be the
ultimate move of this very theism in refusing to privilege man
in any way, since he is not the specific image of any God.

I do not think there is any need to work out for God the place
that awaits him in the midst of the world. With the incarnation,
God came where no room was left for him—either in the continuity of the genealogies of Israel,[9] or in the inn at Bethlehem
(Luke 2. 7). God comes and makes his living intervention in the
very place where the God concept has fallen into disuse, impossibility and uselessness. In what follows, I do not intend to use
the God concept as an apologetic ploy but to try to understand
the more adequate comprehension of God to be obtained from a
cultural situation that rejects so many images traditionally connected with the God concept.

The God concept was traditionally linked with the grounding
and justification of that which is—the *status quo*. God assured
permanence where man installed contingency. In amalgamating
the Hebrew notion of faith throughout the generations and the
ages with the Greek concept of an absolute freed from lack and
need, theology forged a concept of God in which there was a
predominance of eternity opposed to time and of non-temporality
to history. But the concept of this particular God has always been
difficult to reconcile with the innovative interventions which the
God of the Bible brings about in time and by means of which

[9] This seems to me to be the theological meaning of the so-called "virgin"
birth—i.e., the insistence on the non-legitimacy of Mary, who was not mar-
ried to Joseph, rather than on the supernatural miracle of Jesus' birth; cf.
Matthew 1. 18, and Luke 3. 23.

he initiates events which compromise him. One must ask whether man is not the ground of a permanence, and God (on the contrary) the irruption of a contingency. Paradoxically, it is necessary to reverse the direction of Sartre's argument, and to ask whether God is not best characterized by the attributes which Sartre asserts pertain to man: that is, the breaching of consciousness and of a plan in the opacity of the world and of things. It is necessary to speak anthropologically (but not anthropocentrically) of God in order to distinguish him "theologically"—in the form of permanence and regularity, as the new form of knowledge speaks of man. We now have to oppose to a once more essentialist man an existentialist concept of God, if the biblical God is in fact the one who gives himself to be known in the innovative and initiatory acts of exodus and resurrection. If man is the permanent do-it-yourself constructor of mythic, institutional and logical mediations between contrary data which are actually irreconcilable other than by means of imaginary compromises, God shows himself (as against that man) as the one who unmakes former facts and posits new ones. Man is the *"bricoleur"* of his permanence; God the creator of his contingency.

By "contingency", I mean that which is unforeseeable and irregular, that which acts contrary to determinations and organizations. And the most striking feature of the God of the Bible is precisely that, in contradistinction to the gods of the religions round about Israel, he did not reproduce the regularities of social practice. For example, he is not the god of vegetation cycles, of fertility rhythms, of planetary repetitions, or of annual celebrations of power—as were the gods of Canaan, Egypt and Assyria. To say of this God that he is unique, signifies of course that his power cannot be compared with that of idols, but also that he reveals himself in unique actions, which the faith of generations will reactualize in their uniqueness, but not repeat as if their validity were exhausted after a certain cycle. When made in the image of nature, man ensures the permanence of his dwelling in the world by incessantly recommencing propitiatory mediations. But when man is made in the image of the contingent interventions of God, he ensures the truth of his faith by returning unceasingly to the unique action which he remembers and hopes in. It is no longer a question of his making himself a ground, but of living the anamnesis and the promise of a contingency. The true countenance of God is not the image of immutability but, on the contrary, that of a novelty. God is the one by whom the new enters into human immutability.

Edmund Leach, one of the English disciples of Lévi-Strauss, has tried to discover the key to the biblical texts concerning the genealogy of Solomon.[10] According to him, these texts offer an imaginary mediation in regard to the intolerable situation in which Israel found itself, i.e., having on theological grounds to refuse mixed marriages with non-Jews, while having on political grounds to live in peace in the midst of largely assimilated neighbours. Leach explains that the editorial amalgam of the texts seeks to resolve the permanent conflict between a theoretical endogamy and a practical exogamy. Hence the permanence of solutions hidden behind the apparent obscurity and disorder of details. Leach offers this interpretation on the basis of a similar problem of kinship in the genealogy of Jesus at the beginning of the gospel according to Matthew. According to him, four "equivocal" women are listed (Tamar, Rahab, Ruth, Uriah's wife—before Mary, who is mentioned after them), without any convincing explanation from any Christian commentator, because (according to Leach) these commentators did not see the permanence of the ethnological problem to which these different genealogical texts try to offer a solution. Nevertheless we must remember that biblical theology always understood these passages as referring not to the human persistence of a problem of kinship, but to the divine contingency of choice. The God who, in his faithfulness to his promise, watches over the genealogies is also the God who incessantly intervenes to refute them. This is why four "irregular" women—or five, including Mary—appear in Jesus' messianic genealogy according to Matthew. They recall the fact that the contingency of God (theologically, the freedom of his grace) always disturbs the mundane genealogies of human permanence. This theological explanation (also concealed) seems to be more convincing than Leach's ethnological explanation, since it is supported by the context as a whole. But, without offering a detailed refutation, I should like above all to show by an example how

[10] Edmund Leach, "The legitimacy of Solomon", in *Genesis as Myth* (London, 1969).

God may be said to be contingency, and man permanence. Where the ethnology of kinship discovers a mediation in a self-made permanence, the theology of divine election finds an incessantly surprising intervention.

The concept of God at the time of a new organizational knowledge and of the one-dimensional society therefore plays a role quite different to that traditionally attributed to it by classical metaphysics. Here God intervenes but does not ground. He upsets systematizing regularity. In the midst of the immutability of time he constitutes the moment of newness. He reveals his name through the anonymity of rules. Thus, and not by means of a mythic curiosity regarding the "how" of the origins, and not by means of apocalyptic speculation on the "how" of the end, God in the midst of time takes the name of creator. God preserves the validity of contingency in depriving it for the sake of faith of its title of chance, and in simultaneously removing the confusion between his fidelity and necessity. God is contingency: that is to say, he is the unforeseeable which establishes. The major aspect of the encounter between God and history is not that history becomes visibly rational and totalizable, but that the new enters history—yet not as a subjective illusion. Ultimately it is to the concept of God that human history must have recourse for an assurance that creativity (and not only a patching together of things permanent) is still possible. Here a strange reversal takes place. God usually appeared as the one who, by means of his creation (supposedly already accomplished), denied human creativity; who, in posing the grounds of being, devalued history; and who, by means of his absolute, killed the vitality of the relative. Today the encounter (if there can be an encounter) operates differently and (in my sense) in a way in which the biblical sources are more justly observed. God appears as the "irregular" aspect of society, as the unforeseeable aspect of history, as the contingency of a grace which is not arbitrary since it bears witness in this very contingency to the freedom of love and not to the chance of indifference.


## III. MEDIATIONS

I mentioned a possible new usage for the God concept. I have tried to show how God would no longer appear as an impossible synthesis of consciousness and the world, of the for-itself and the in-itself, of human time and cosmic atemporality (which is, for instance, what he is in Sartre's ontology), but as the contingent irruption of novelty into the permanence of rules. Of course there are two precautions to be taken here. From the viewpoint of God, his reality is not to be estimated by the rediscovered utility of his concept. From the human viewpoint, there is (in what I have called the new form of knowledge) no call for an absent God who could deregulate systems and initiate surprise. First of all because the new form of knowledge undertakes to re-discover the regularities hidden behind the apparent irruptions (as we have seen in the case of Leach's ethnological interpreta-tion, which replaces a theology of election of which Leach seems in fact unaware. But why call God the "new" on earth? I do not claim to have allowed God a more appropriate location, in trans-ferring his concept from the category of immutable foundation to the category of creative contingency. Apologetics is always at fault if it pleads for something absent rather than bear witness to something present.

Three points seem important:

1. The epistemological surgery at which we have assisted, this sudden deflection of thought from spontaneity, thought and his-tory towards regularity and logic, warns us that theology is not addressed to a culture of the same, unchanging orientation. Yet theology must be aware of the identity of its cultural partners. If the vitality of theology arises from the reality of God, its mobility is always related to cultural developments. I have stressed what theology can assert polemically as against the dominant culture, rather than what it is tempted to reproduce of that culture. In an "existentialist" epoch, the emphasis would have to be on the faithfulness of God's plan. In a "structuralist" epoch, the stress would be instead on the creative novelty of his interventions. The reality of faith does not depend on the more or less favour-able opportunities which culture offers it, but its intelligibility does depend on adequate perception of its proper direction. If the cultural perspective is subject to a "see-saw" effort, theology has to take this into account. Its concept of God must also be re-oriented. This is all the more important when, as at present, the

cultural situation is by no means clear, and theology suffers from this confusion.[11]

2. Although I have distinguished the reality of God from the possible utility of the concept of God, I believe that what happens to that concept is of major importance from the human point of view. A God who is real but not "used" in thought becomes an ineffable God. He withdraws from reflective thought into an incommunicable intimism. The christological concentration that allowed some people to believe they could dispense with a theological formulation is not an issue here. Christology is annunciation of the true name of God and not a disallowal of its use. What is sometimes known as "christological atheism" amounts to a Jesus-centrism which sheds no decisive light on God or on man. In christology the addition of logic to the designation of Christ in Jesus shows that the question of the God concept and of its use also depends on the reality of the presence of the living God. The reality always precedes the concept: without this truth we would make God dependent on the cognitive possibilities of our intellects.

3. We have today to insist on God as a *surprising contingency*; but this does not mean that God is outside the category of repetition. A thinker of as existentialist a cast as Kierkegaard saw repetition as a fundamental category for faith. Without repetition, in fact, faith is incapable of understanding how contingency does not merely carry on discarding the old in order to project itself towards an increasingly unattainable and imaginary new. The contingency of God institutes the new, and lays down the rules of the new. In this sense it is a creative and not only an assertive, an innovative and not only an insurrectionary contingency. God's protest does not condemn his freedom to perpetual banishment. God's liberty, in becoming incarnate, creates novelty in actuality. It is a beginning, and not a refurbishing of the old; but it is also a new beginning in the old and not a continual futurism. God protests by instituting the new: by means of the contingency of his liberty, and for man's benefit.

*Translated by John Griffiths*

[11] One of the first articles to have systematized the reversal of tendencies would seem to be Lawrence Rosen's "Language, history and the logic of inquiry in Lévi-Strauss and Sartre", in *History and Theory*, 1971, Vol. 10, No. 3, pp. 269–94. Unfortunately his conclusion is eclectic and deceptive.

Claude Geffré

# Non-Metaphysical Theology

Pascal's attack on the God of the philosophers is more relevant than ever. This is not simply because of an irreducible character attached to the experience of the living God of faith; theological language about God is being subjected to a radical critique as part of a general crisis of metaphysical language and arguments. The theologians themselves eagerly echo such phrases as "the end of metaphysics", "the death of the God of metaphysics", "the end of theism" and "the beginning of a post-metaphysical age". Some, far from taking fright at this collapse of traditional metaphysics, greet it as a liberating event for Christian theology. The suspect alliance between the God of the philosophers and the God of Jesus Christ is at last broken, and the theologian is finally free to say what he has been entrusted with by revelation. In this view the term "non-metaphysical theology" emphasizes one of the most promising characteristics of the theology of the future.

All this is part of a fundamental debate which includes in the first place an historical dimension concerned with the relations between the God of philosophy and the God of Christian theology in the history of Western thought. It includes, however, a philosophical dimension concerned with the nature of theological language in its relation to the actual experience of the believer. It is impossible to consider all the elements of this debate in this article; I want merely to remove some ambiguities in facile talk about "non-metaphysical theology". The expression has a legitimate sense if it is used to denounce the false objectifications of metaphysical theology or the privileged connection of theology with any particular metaphysics, but it is an empty phrase if it is used to mean that we can give up the ontological reference of theological language as a language about God.

I shall begin by looking at the critique of metaphysical language formulated by the representatives of radical, or "death-of-God", theology. I shall then ask what should be our attitude to the critique of *onto-theology*, as the hidden essence of traditional metaphysical theology. This will lead to a consideration of the attack on the objectivity of God by a certain theological existentialism. I then examine the new paths open to a non-metaphysical theology.

## I. The Crisis of Language about God

In different ways, every death-of-God theologian is under the influence of the analytic philosophy of the Vienna Circle or of the Oxford school of "linguistic analysis", and asserts that metaphysical propositions are strictly speaking meaningless. We may quote the following characteristic lines of Wittgenstein's: "Most of the propositions and questions to be found in philosophical works are not false but nonsensical... Most of the propositions and questions of philosophers arise from our failure to understand the logic of our language."[1]

But, for my present purpose, it is above all important to note that in the whole current of radical theology the old debate about the relation between the God of metaphysics and the God of faith has been completely overtaken. It is the very word "God" which lacks meaning. Van Buren, for example, can write: "Today we can no longer even understand Nietzsche's cry 'God is dead'.... The problem is that, for us, the word 'God' is dead." The question is therefore not about the possibility of metaphysical language about God. It is the much more radical question about the very possibility of language about God, whether this language is metaphysical or religious. Culturally, the death of metaphysics simply preceded the death of God in the history of Western thought, and the theologians of the death of God con-

---

[1] L. Wittgenstein, *Tractatus Logico-Philosophicus*, new translation by D. F. Pears and B. F. McGuinness (London and New York, 1961), 4003.

sider these two cultural events as identical symptoms of the "radically secular nature" of our culture.

One of the signs of this radical attitude is that for contemporary analytical philosophers the problem is no longer one of the *validity* of metaphysical or theological statements but one of their meaning.[2] For the atheist and even for the agnostic, the question of God still has a meaning, but for the neo-positivist analytical philosophy the very word "God" lacks meaning. Indeed, if the "verification principle" provides a criterion for distinguishing meaningful propositions, any proposition in which God occurs as subject is not even false but meaningless. It is very apt to talk of a "semantic atheism" distinct from classical forms of atheism.[3]

We thus have to understand the "death-of-God" theology as a desperate attempt to maintain a Christian theological language when the impossibility of a meaningful language about God has been accepted as an inescapable cultural fact. In the face of such a theology, the real debate is not about the legitimacy of a non-metaphysical theology but about whether it is possible at all to have a Christian theology which no longer mentions God. In our view a Christian theology *without* God is a nonsense, or at least it is no more than a form of anthropology. It is possible to show that it is contradictory to continue to appeal to the lordship of Christ over the world and man, and at the same time to assert the total self-sufficiency of secular man and his inability to state the problem of God.

In fact, the most recent representatives of analytical philosophy, in particular those who take their inspiration from the later Wittgenstein, show an increasing interest in the study of religious language. They reject quite specifically the narrowness of the "verification principle" and believe that there are affirmations about reality which are totally meaningful even though they cannot be empirically verified. This is true, for example, in the moral and religious orders. In so far as it is an element of human behaviour, language shares its complexity. There are dif-

[2] Cf. Landon Gilkey, *Naming the Whirlwind: The Renewal of God-Language* (New York, 1969), pp. 13–25.
[3] The expression "semantic atheism" is used by D. Antiseri in *Foi sans métaphysique ni théologie* (Paris, 1970), p. 32.

ferent "language games" which cannot be reduced to a single form. The "language game" to which the word "God" belongs is religion. We must certainly reformulate our language about God to take account of the limits of secular man's understanding, but if we can no longer talk about God then we cannot talk about the rest of religion.

If we admit that there can be meaningful accounts of reality which cannot be empirically verified, why deny that religious language in general and language about God in particular can be meaningful? To refuse to reduce the language to empirical accounts is to admit the possibility of *metaphysical* language. From the philosopher's point of view, theological language is necessarily metaphysical, at least in the very general sense that it is not empirically verifiable. The phrase "non-metaphysical theology" can mean a theology which does not use metaphysical categories and is not tied to a particular system of metaphysics. But, having regard to a criteriology of languages, theological language belongs to the category of metaphysical, or at least speculative, language in the sense that it is *transgressive* with regard to the immediate data of experience and bears, in principle, on a reality which is accessible only through an interpretation.[4]

## II. The Critique of Onto-theology

The "death-of-God" movement in theology is merely the most radical expression of the fundamental crisis facing contemporary theology. But in order to understand and assess the attempt to create a non-metaphysical Christian theology we must take account of Heidegger's critique of onto-theology, which is seen as the hidden essence of Western metaphysics. It is obviously possible to dispute the interpretation of the historical destiny of Western metaphysics put forward by Heidegger, but it would be impossible to spend too much time in considering the fact that for the first time in the history of Christian thought in the West we are in a philosophical situation which allows us seriously to question the association of the "metaphysical" and the "theological" in Christian theology.

[4] Cf. J. Ladrière, "Théologie et langage de l'intérpretation", *Rev. théol. de Louvain* 1 (1970), p. 258.

According to Heidegger, the cultural death of God conceived of as an object is written into the very destiny of metaphysics from its origin. In fact it is the same movement in metaphysics which makes God the absolute foundation of existence and kills him. Right from the start metaphysics has been unable to ask questions about the totality of existence without immediately postulating a supreme existence as the basis of being. This desire to find a foundation deeper than given existence shows rational man's desire for representation. The hidden essence of traditional metaphysics is onto-theology, that is to say, the explanation of an existence by its being and of being by a supreme existence: "An existence is understood in terms of its reasons for being, in order that, being understood, it may come into man's power."[5] Greek metaphysics did not become "onto-theology" because it was absorbed into Christian theology; it was onto-theology from the start.

In the modern era, absolute Spirit and, finally, man have replaced God understood as the supreme Existence. In Hegel the spirit of man tends to become the spirit of God, and in Nietzsche we reach the murder of God by the self-foundation of the will to power. This reversal was possible because right from the beginning God was thought of as existence which man could control by representing. The fact of man's replacing God as the foundation is written into the movement of metaphysics itself in the form of the desire to explain the totality of the real by transcending it from a foundation.

This identification of the aim of Western metaphysics as a desire to explain, under the sign of the logos, invites us to undertake a critical re-reading of traditional theology as metaphysical theology. The history of Christian theology is in fact inseparable from the history of conceptions of being. And today the crisis of metaphysics in Heidegger's sense begins a new era for Christian theology, in which it is no longer possible to confuse the elements of theology deriving strictly from God, and those deriving from nature on a purely ontological level. In other words, theology is invited to be itself and to say what it has been given to say by

[5] O. Pöggeler, *La Pensée de Martin Heidegger* (Paris, 1967), p. 384 (*Der Denkweg Martin Heideggers*: Pfüllingen, 1963).

revelation.[6] This is all the easier today, since the valuable work of biblical research is helping us to understand more and more clearly the specific originality of the Judaeo-Christian God.

The theology of Thomas Aquinas remains an unparalleled achievement of Christian theology in the form of metaphysical theology. In interpreting the God who revealed himself to Moses in terms of being, Aquinas bridged the gulf between faith and knowledge and showed that the biblical God was identical with the God reached by the rational approach of the philosophers. Moreover, Aquinas' approach is thoroughly theological; he did not begin by working out an idea of God which he later identified with the God of revelation.[7] Nevertheless, by making the supreme Being the intelligible principle which made it possible to take account of all the attributes and works of God, Aquinas took a decision which was to have serious consequences for the future of Christian thought. In our effort to take seriously the relation of God to the history of salvation, we are even more aware to-day of the risks inherent in such a theological attempt. It may even be asked whether an ontological theology of this sort does not bear in itself in germ the danger of the false objectification of God which is the triumph of natural reason. In other words, does such a theology escape the destiny of Western metaphysics as Heidegger understands it? It seems hard to deny that Aquinas's science of theology is part of the onto-theological enterprise of metaphysics. In the first place it derives the truth of existences from the primary truth of their principle, absolute Being, and it also tries to make sense of, to explain, revealed mysteries on the basis of God understood as the cause and foundation of all that exists. The *Ipsum Esse subsistens* becomes the hermeneutic principle of all theology.

Even in the case of God's being, being is still thought of as the being of an existence. God is the first existence, *primum Ens.*

---

[6] I have explained my ideas on this new age in theology at greater length in my study "L'objectivité propre au Dieu révélé", in *L'analyse du langage théologique. Le nom de Dieu* (Paris, 1969), pp. 403–21.

[7] Cf. Cl. Geffré, "Théologie naturelle et révélation dans la connaissance du Dieu un", in *L'existence de Dieu*, Cahiers de l'actualité religieuse 16 (Paris, 1963), pp. 297–317, and B. Montagnes, "Le Dieu de la philosophie et le Dieu de la foi", in *Procès de l'objectivité de Dieu* (Paris, 1969), pp. 215–31.

This is very definitely representational thought in Heidegger's sense, thought which stands over against what it thinks and makes it present to itself. If this metaphysical thought is the inevitable destiny of being, we can even say (with Welte) that Aquinas's metaphysics "developed what was for its time the highest form of metaphysics, the influence of which was to extend for a long time, perhaps even throughout the time of the domination of metaphysics".[8] And if there was in fact in Aquinas "the seed of the possibility of going beyond metaphysics", that is, a very clear realization of how much of the divine *Ipsum Esse* lay beyond conceptualization, this remained in the background: the later development of Thomist thought was affected by the increasing tendency to conceptualization.

The task of Christian theology at the end of metaphysics is therefore to make clear the hidden essence of the enterprise of metaphysical theology, its desire to explain revelation by starting from God conceived as the absolute foundation of existence. In metaphysical theology there is a rigorous reduction of the biblical attributes of God, particularly when they are expressed in verbal form, to the pure actuality of Being. This leads to inescapable difficulties if we really want to take seriously the "historical" actions of God (the creation, incarnation and divinization). The limitation of a metaphysical theology based solely on the analogy of being, with its strict distinction between proper and metaphorical divine names is that it ignores the intelligibility proper to the great biblical symbols. The identity of God with absolute Being then becomes the ultimate criterion for the validity of language about God. This involves the risk of keeping only those elements of biblical language about God which can be formulated in the conceptual system of scientific theology. Aquinas, for example, tries to understand the history of salvation by starting from the necessary properties of God understood as absolute Being, but he does not show enough of the new understanding of the transcendence of God as love which is made available to us by the history of salvation. So in metaphysical theology, the triumph of explanatory thought, everything happens as if the

[8] B. Welte, "La métaphysique de S. Thomas d'Aquin et la pensée de l'histoire de l'être chez Heidegger", *Revue des sciences philosophiques et théologiques* 50 (1965), p. 612.

deepest mystery of the God who reveals himself were "reduced" to a pre-existing foundation, derived ultimately from the logos of human reason. The legitimate ambition of a non-metaphysical theology would be to accept "reduction to mystery", that is, to think about the mystery of God only within the coming of truth which is revelation.

### III. The Attack on the Objectivity of God

The realization of the hidden essence of metaphysical theology is inseparable from the critique of the objectivity of God in contemporary theology. Particularly within Protestant theology, there has been for half a century a radical critique of objective knowledge of God.[9] This radical critique is in continuity with Luther's protest against scholastic theology, but Barth and Bultmann are, each in his own way, heirs of the Kantian critique. They both want to go beyond the objectivism of metaphysical theology and to abandon the subject-object schema. Since Kant, God-language has lost its ontological roots, and it is impossible to make the God of practical reason into an objective reality.[10]

For Barth, God is the basis of his own objectivity in so far as, through revelation, he gratuitously becomes an object of knowledge and love. For Bultmann, the objectification of God in the metaphysical form of traditional theology is the same procedure as that of mythical thought, which would control God by talking of the beyond in the categories of this world. Any objective language about God is necessarily idolatrous because we cannot speak of God beyond what reaches us here and now in the decision of faith. The only way in which I can respect God's objectivity is to allow myself to be transformed by him in the obedience of faith instead of making him present to me as a represented object.

This desire to go beyond the objectivism of traditional theology is common to many present-day developments in theology,

[9] Cf. A. Dumas, "La critique de l'objectivité de Dieu dans la théologie protestante", in *Procès de l'objectivité de Dieu, op. cit.*, pp. 147–68.

[10] See W. Schulz's *Der Gott der neuzeitlichen Metaphysik* (Pfüllingen, 1967). Schulz has shown brilliantly how God in the modern age has become the medium and the condition of possibility for man's spiritual fulfilment.

whether in so-called existentialist theology or in theological personalism. But, in the light of the fate of metaphysics, we may ask if this attack on the objectivity of God is not secretly related to the same enterprise of metaphysical theology, its desire for explanations. Put another way, is not this trend in theology, which is trying to come to terms with the irreducible event of revelation by starting from man defined as existence instead of from man defined as a rational animal, itself still to some extent dominated by the subjectivity of man?

In the face of this tendency of non-metaphysical theology, it is sometimes rightly asked whether God is still known in himself. If we speak of God in terms of a call, surely we reduce him to the pure paradox of a confrontation with man? If God is reduced to the occurrence of an encounter which changes me, the content of God is of little importance; he still has his regulative function. We have replaced the God of metaphysics by the God of the ethical conscience: God understood as absolute demands and the regulating principle of human action. We may therefore put the question: When theological existentialism no longer dares to objectify God in order to preserve his inexpressible character, does it not reduce God to the meaning he has for man? If this is so, existentialist theology, trying to be non-metaphysical in order the better to respect the particular originality of the God of faith, is in fact evidence for the anthropological orientation of theology in modern times. We are witnessing the end of the existentialization and interiorization of the faith which began with Luther and in which Feuerbach saw an "anthropocentric" shift.[11] It is also significant that in Catholicism and Protestantism today there is a reaction against the idealism and individualism of existentialist hermeneutics, and a new emphasis on the historical basis of Christianity. The new theologies of history (Moltmann and, especially, Pannenberg) reject a starting-point for the search for God in the immanence of thought, and look for a hermeneutic criterion in universal history, seen as the revelation of God.

An accurate description of the real situation of contemporary theology in its role as talk about God would seem to be given in the following question: At the moment when the God-concept,

[11] Cf. K. Löwith, *From Hegel to Nietzsche* (London, 1969), Chapter 5 (*Von Hegel zu Nietzsche*, Zürich, 1941).

the object of traditional metaphysics, is dead, how can we overcome theological objectivism without falling into the anthropocentrism of existentialist theologies? To conclude, I would simply like to suggest the most promising directions for a non-metaphysical Christian theology which would retain its speculative ambitions.

## IV. The Non-Metaphysical Theology of the Future

Theology as the science of faith must work out its own way of handling concepts. It is concerned with an historical revelation which is accessible only in faith and has at its disposal a certain number of basic concepts with an essential relation to the historical event of salvation. The appropriation of these basic concepts by the understanding is, however, never complete. The permanent task of theology as an attempt to understand faith will be to work out a new language always based on the basic concepts of revelation but trying to go beyond them in an effort to make the content of faith more intelligible at a given moment of history. Since the realities of faith are by definition accessible only through an interpretation, the language of theology will inevitably be a speculative language in the sense that it goes beyond the limits of descriptive language. In its effort to work out a new speculative language, Christian theology will make privileged use of the resources of philosophical language, but it is not tied to any specific conceptual system. Even if theology cannot abandon the ontological content of its statements, it is free in relation to the categories and movement of thought of traditional metaphysics.

It is this freedom which the theology of the future is trying to demonstrate by its claim to be non-metaphysical. Christian theology today is trying to escape from the double impasse of theological objectivism and theological existentialism which we have discussed. The third way must be that of a non-objectifying speculative theology which can escape from the destiny of metaphysics as seen by Heidegger. Theology cannot abandon its speculative and systematic ambitions, but it must be able to use its freedom to say what it has been given to say by revelation. A theology which abandons the movement of thought within metaphysical thought will not try to objectify God by identifying him with the supreme Being, the basis of all existence. But for all that God is not a pure "It", and not the other party without content in an encounter about which nothing can be said. In this search for a non-objectifying ontological language the theologian can find extremely valuable philosophical material in the later Heidegger's "ontology of language", and in particular in his meditation on "saying as a part of being" or, better, "being's claim on saying".[12] "What language says is not necessarily the formulation of propositions *about* objects. In its depths language is the expression of what reveals itself and addresses itself to man in many ways, to the extent that man does not close himself to what is disclosed by means of the domination of objectifying thought and by restricting himself to this."[13]

Heidegger himself would reject any use of his philosophy in theology, but we may ask, following Ott, if it is not possible to re-examine the relation of theological thought to revelation in the light of the new questioning of being which Heidegger initiated. Just as there is a "topology of being", or a special place where the truth of being is disclosed, there is also a special place in which the truth which is the source of revelation allows itself to be appropriated by the believer. Our task therefore must be to begin a movement of thought in theology which will appropriate revealed truth by starting from its special place instead of trying to explain the irreducible mystery of God by starting from a pre-existing basis, whether it is God as Absolute Being or man in his self-understanding.[14] The privileged place for talk about God is the economy of the incarnate Word. We cannot start from an existing idea of God and then see how it is modified by the event of the incarnation. We can only know the God of Jesus Christ by starting from the particular history of Jesus. The Christian God is not an "object" in the sense of a *Gegenstand*,

[12] I have taken these expressions from Paul Ricoeur's preface to the French translation of Bultmann's *Jesus* (Paris, 1968, p. 28).

[13] M. Heidegger, "Quelques indications sur des points de vue principaux du colloque théologique consacré au 'Problème d'une pensée et d'un langage non-objectivants dans la théologie d'aujourd'hui' ", unpublished text of 1964 in *Archives de Philosophie* 32 (1969), p. 413.

[14] On the movement of thought in non-metaphysical theology, see my "L'objectivité propre au Dieu révélé", *art. cit.*, pp. 413 ff.

something which can be controlled. He has the objectivity of a personal mystery. If non-metaphysical theology is faithful to the place which is our starting-point in appropriating the truth of revelation, it will go beyond not only the subject-object schema but the representative schema of an interpersonal "I-Thou" relation between man and God.

Non-metaphysical theology, rooted in the economy, will continue to conceive of God as being, but no longer in the categories of idea, substance and nature. It will think of him in the categories of history and eschatology, and will try in this way to express the ontological primacy of the future over the present in the divine Being. Eternity will now no longer be a negative property, the absence of time; it will describe God's control over the future. If the future is the mode of being most appropriate to the biblical God, we can see that he cannot be captured by the objectifications of theism, and that no event in the history of salvation (not even the resurrection of Christ) can exhaust his promises. The truth of talk about God will be much more gradual anticipation and manifestation than *adaequatio* in relation to an immutable essence. And history is less the epiphany through time of the eternal presence of God than the gradual accomplishment of a future which is always unknown and will not be disclosed until the end of history, but opens each present moment on to the future.

We can now see that non-metaphysical theology is not just one more anti-philosophical slogan. It is the demand for a theology which will at last be "theological". The theology of the future will still be an ontological theology, but will aim at being a *theology of reality*. Going beyond the metaphysical dualism of God and the world, it will have to work towards a better understanding of how Jesus Christ is the unity of the reality of God and the reality of the world.

*Translated by Francis McDonagh*

# PART II
## BULLETIN

Karel Skalický

# "God is not quite dead": Marxists on the God Question

AT THE beginning of the sixties Lobkowicz could write: "There has never been an independent Czechoslovak Marxism-Leninism; there is only one Marxism-Leninism, the Soviet one."[1] But today, at the beginning of the seventies, we must admit that this is no longer true. During the sixties Marxist philosophy produced a comparative abundance of philosophical works differing from the official orthodoxy.

A progressive liberalization provided a suitable climate in which this movement could not fail to find expression and which was reflected even in theoretical conceptions of the "ideological struggle against religion". The two Marxist philosophers who paid the closest attention to the "religious question" were Milan Machovec and Vitěslav Gardavský; the first was a Marxist of the older generation, the second was a younger man who entered the field of philosophy only in the nineteen-sixties, and this is why, so it would seem, that tactical considerations had no influence on him. His thinking therefore gives a clearer picture of the development of theory in regard to the problem of religion. In my view it is a typical example of the spiritual evolution of the whole middle generation of Czechslovak Marxists.

Gardavský, a militant Communist, at first concerned himself mainly with political problems. In his first book, *Phenomenon Germania*,[2] he concentrated his attention on German Christian

[1] N. Lobkowicz, *Marxismus-Leninismus in der ČSR* (Dordrecht, 1961), p. xiii.
[2] Original title: *Fenoméne Nemecko* (Prague, 1967).

Democracy, that is, on the Catholic attitude to industrial society,
face to face with the Marxist conception of Communism. Having
regard to the purpose of this article, I shall mention only three
of Gardavský's ideas which he puts forward in this work, and
which seem worth considering for the importance they have for
his thought as a whole.

1. The Church, Gardavský says, *is not bourgeois* in its origins.[3]

2. It is because of this non-bourgeois character that we are
able to discover the internal contradictions inherent in bourgeois
democracy. The contradiction is that capitalist society has provided the material conditions for all men to live a truly human
life ("for the universality of mankind"[4]), whereas, by its class
structure, by its own particular structure, "it creates a situation
of complete alienation for men".[5] This contradiction, however,
in the Church's view, constitutes "a denial of the fact that it de-
fends private property as a natural right". To the Church this
looks like a contradiction between power and authority,[6] since for
the Church bourgeois democracy is merely a regime "based on
power but lacking authority within itself".[7] The "Catholic attitude" therefore strives (according to Gardavský, in vain) on a
universal scale to overcome the class structure of bourgeois democracy. This is the link with Marx's Communism that allows,
under certain conditions, as Gardavský says in conclusion, "a
relative convergence of the two".[8]

This unusual view, expressed by a militant Communist, does
not, it would appear, go beyond a superficial criticism confined
to looking on Catholicism as "in practice, a force in contemporary society";[9] the ideas in question do not rise above the level
of politics.

In his second book, *God is not Quite Dead*,[10] the author's per-

---

[3] *Op. cit.*, p. 109.
[4] *Op. cit.*, p. 108.
[5] *Ibid.*
[6] *Op. cit.*, p. 109
[7] *Op. cit.*, p. 108.
[8] *Op. cit.*, p. 211.
[9] *Op. cit.*, p. 80.
[10] Original title: *Buh není zcela mrtev* (Prague, 1967). For a more detailed analysis of the book see my article, "A Czechoslovak Marxist and
the Death of God", in *Filosofia e Vita*, 4 (1969), pp. 90–102.

spective is broader and the comparison more profound. But now the writer does not merely compare two kinds of society; his reflections are concerned with deeper problems. It is true that, here too, the problem of theism and atheism is considered in political terms, but the writer gives it another dimension by emphasizing its roots in history: "Although our attitude to Christianity will still be mainly *political*, this does not mean that we are precluded from asking whether Christianity has any significance for Socialism";[11] and, if so, "in what sense". Now it is precisely in his historical comparison of Marxism with Christianity that Gardavský seems to realize that there is something lacking in Marxism, a lack which he calls "an inadequate appreciation of historical foundations". This, according to him, is because Communism, after so many decades of struggle, can be seen, and is seen by many, as something extraneous to history; something experimental and conditional, destined to disappear within a short time, like so many other doctrines, because it has not succeeded in "taking deep roots in the soil of European and world history".[12] At the back of this historical interest a deeper interest manifests itself, which we might call "metaphysical". Gardavský perceives that Christianity continues to be indispensable for so many, including Socialists, because it provides a response to men's most profound aspirations and questions—although up to now it has been ignored and disregarded by official Marxism-Leninism. Accordingly, the writer asks himself: "What, then, is God? Where are the gaps in Socialism? Why this silence of Marxism in the face of such questions? Where, in our ideology, are those greater depths shown in Christianity? What are the motives which might impel a man to fight for the realization of Socialism with greater force than that which faith in God provides?"[13] In addition to the insufficient "roots in history", Gardavský also notes another gap which may perhaps be characterized as an "absence of a deeper human dimension".

In the first part of his book, Gardavský is entirely concerned to discover the Christian historical inheritance and the situation of present-day theology. This argument is the weakest part of the

[11] *Op. cit.*, p. 16.
[12] *Op. cit.*, p. 13.
[13] *Op. cit.*, p. 16.

whole book and does not come within the purpose of this article.
The most interesting section begins with reflections on atheism.
Gardavský refuses especially to identify himself with militant
atheism, "with its illusions, its over-simplification and its
errors",[14] which for the most part are the result of a method of
thinking brought about by the Stalinist reduction of dialectical
materialism to a pre-Marxist mechanical materialism.[15] He rejects
this, not with the intention of weakening Marxism, but, on the
contrary, with the aim of discovering the authentic inspiration
of Marxism. For him, atheism is "essentially the framework of
Marxist thought, where the Marxist poses questions and demands
responses".[16] "It is the radical form of the Marxist *Weltan-
schauung*."[17] "Atheism", Gardavský argues, "is not merely acci-
dental in Marxism, but may be considered as the primary philosophy of Marxism, Marxism's metaphysics."[18]

But what does Gardavský mean by metaphysics? He explains
(undoubtedly inspired here by Garaudy) thus: "Mankind is developing, transcending itself, changing within its natural limits
to its historical limits, as a result of manifold practical activities.
Metaphysics is the reflection, or rather the theory of this active
process; it deals with a subjectivity that rises above itself."[19] This
metaphysics is implicit in Marx's works, but, according to Gardavský, is obscured by the concrete necessities of the class-struggle,
and has to be re-stated.[20] He foresees that we are "at the beginning
of an intellectual task of enormous importance, and fundamental
significance in the evolution of Marxism, for the increase of its
attraction and its achievement of its long-range social aims".[21]
Gardavský is very well aware of the vastness of this undertaking,
but restricts his reflections to the problem of the future and the
problem of death.

The problem of the future is considered first of all in the form
of an objection, often found among young people: "Why must

[14] *Op. cit.*, pp. 145, 147.
[15] *Op. cit.*, p. 147.
[16] *Op. cit.*, p. 188.
[17] *Op. cit.*, p. 148.
[18] *Op. cit.*, p. 188.
[19] *Op. cit.*, p. 190.
[20] *Op. cit.*, p. 191.
[21] *Ibid*.

we spend so much of our lives in the service of an idea, that is, of Communism? Is it only so that our sons and our sons' sons may have better lives? Why should we take into consideration something that does not yet exist, and which we are not certain will ever come into existence, and think of it as more real and important than that which exists here and now? Isn't this utopian? Are we not replacing one faith with another?"[22]

At the basis of this objection, as Gardavský observes, is a more fundamental problem: "What will come about after Communism?"[23] It is clear that if Communism is made something relative, the motive of an unconditional personal endeavour to turn it into reality is paralysed. If, on the other hand, Communism retains its absolute values, the reality is turned into a mere instrument. In this dilemma Gardavský takes his stand "against the absolute validity of Communism". "Neither Socialism nor Communism can be regarded as absolute ends, in the sense that everything becomes only an instrument for turning them into reality...."[24] But in this case we are compelled to ask whether we have before us a history that is a kind of road without an ending (what Bloch calls "an infernal dizziness"). This is what appears to be the case. But at least Gardavský does not console himself (and it is precisely at just this point that he might do so) with Bloch's ontology (with which perhaps he is not acquainted), of "not-yet-being", and the dialectical process he envisages as tending towards the *Novum Ultimum*. Instead he poses the questions: "Where can we find the strength, the vigilance, the courage for action when it appears that every step forward increases the general uneasiness? How can we hold back that flood of destructive scepticism, that terrible indifference which says "I only live once, I live only in the present"?[25]

Here his answer is rather disillusioning. He consoles himself with the fact that "a movement exists, an *avant-garde* which from its beginning was well aware of the provisional character of the situation against which it wages a continual struggle" (he does not say precisely what this *avant-garde* is and what the

[22] *Op. cit.*, p. 192.
[23] *Op. cit.*, p. 191.
[24] *Op. cit.*, p. 198.
[25] *Op. cit.*, p. 194.

struggle against the "provisional" consists of. He singles out the motives for which mankind can undertake such an active commitment not in Messianism, not in "the utopian faith in Communism",[26] but within man himself, "in his awareness of what man is and what he may come to be, to whom is to be given the title of man".[27] But surely these motives, whose foundation is man himself, are harshly denied by the fact of death?

Gardavský tries to meet this problem with his second reflection. Two certainties man has about himself represent the starting-point of his observation: (1) man is a social being capable of transcending himself; (2) man is certain of his death. These two certainties, according to him, have a mutual influence on each other. "Because I am mortal, I am social; society can live and evolve, become more human, because its individual members die ...".[28] But at the same time there is a profound contradiction between these two certainties: "Death takes everything from me, even my very self, but society lives on. Its life, in so far as it is burdened with the death of its individual members, is never totally guaranteed, and is therefore never completed. My death, though it is for me the death of my hopes, is hope for others, hope for society. And vice versa: the life of society is for this very reason a continual overcoming of disillusionment and despair".[28a]

But isn't this easy escapism? An expression, in more involved terms, of that old and well-known consolation: I die, but society will live on? Gardavský attempts to avoid this objection by emphasizing the serious and tragic aspect of individual deaths. But at the same time he wants to persuade us that this tragic quality is derived entirely from the social nature of mankind.[29] Thus he sees the tragedy of death as inherent in the contradiction between the individual and society, while to us it seems that it should be seen in relation to a far more profound contradiction, between being and not-being. If death is considered in the context of the contradiction "individual-society", the escapism consisting in the fact that the individual dies but society continues to live is un-

---

[26] Ibid.
[27] Ibid.
[28] Op. cit., p. 195.
[28a] Ibid.
[29] Op. cit., p. 196.

exceptionable, but its seriousness is unduly diminished. Gardavský does not, however, wish to minimize the seriousness of the death of individuals. He wishes to see it in all its bitterness and tragic quality, and for this reason he is not satisfied with the response, "the individual dies but society goes on living". On the other hand it would seem that he refuses to consider death in the context of the contradiction between "being and not-being", which is the only way death can reveal itself in all its truly tragic character. And so Gardavský, while on the one hand he implicitly refuses to look on death as something wholly and exclusively comprised in the relation individual-society, on the other hand he does not succeed in rising above this condition. Here, in my opinion, lies the contradiction of which he has become the victim. Moreover, he himself concludes his reflections with words which, it seems, reveal his intellectual embarrassment: "We shall", he writes, "be defeated at the end, but we shall not deprive those who survive us of anything that makes up the drama, the struggle, the conflict, of the life of the community, including its final loss. We shall not deprive them of the hope in the development of a community worthy for man to live in. This hope we call Communism. This is our reason for not believing in God, in spite of the fact that this may be absurd."[30]

I would ask if this is not to fall, in a different fashion, into the same absoluteness of Communism which had been refuted a little earlier. "God is not quite dead." What is the meaning of this phrase? The sense of the writer's words may be summed up as follows: God is not wholly dead in so far as the question is about an ideology which, in the condition of our own time, still exerts a cultural, social and political influence which cannot be set aside and which has the capacity to reform itself so as to maintain its influence and even increase it. Apart from this significant interpretation it seems to me that beneath Gardavský's language there is another meaning: The God of the Christians is not such an absurd idea as the Marxists have believed. In our present-day world, unstable, provisional and oppressive, it represents, for those who believe in him, a "centre of security" which is capable of giving sense to human existence, liable as it is to be swept away

[30] *Op. cit.*, p. 202.

by the inconstant floods of history, continually threatened by and at last overcome by death. For this reason the idea of God seems to Gardavský less absurd.

In his third book, *The Sceptic's Hope*,[31] Gardavský's confrontation with the idea of God goes even deeper. Marxism, if it aspires to become a truly universal humanism, must shed its undeniably European character; it must come face to face with something more than the idealism of traditional philosophy. In fact, the dilemma of idealism-materialism is not deep enough, for it emerges as a stream of contradictions bound up with bourgeois philosophy (begun by Descartes) and based on the "active idea"[32] of man's independence and his dominance over nature. Gardavský therefore examines the postulate of "bourgeois heroism", comparing it with the practical idea inherent in medieval theology, which (according to him) would consist in a quite different idea: in a denial of independence (a sense of sin) in men, who are helpless when face to face with nature.[33] Both practical ideas have one thing in common, "in their basic features the one, like the other, has a conception of the way in which to articulate given space",[34] in the manner "in which man should be able to exert his power over the world of space".[35] But this idea is inherited from mythology and Greek thought (not so much from medieval theology, as from the science of the Renaissance which goes back to Aristotle and Plato). This idea is in sharp contrast with the substance of the "Judaeo-Christian myth", which seeks to liberate man not in relation to man's nature, but in the creative activity aroused in us by our relations with our fellow men. The difference is put back still further, right back to mythological sources, "starting from which has come a crystallization of the practical idea of man's power over space, and a reply to the question of who man is and in what his power consists".[36] Marxism is thus brought face to face with myth. "It is", Gardavský writes,

[31] Original title, *Naděje ze skepse*, Dialogue 9 (Prague, 1969).

[32] For Gardavský the "practical idea" is a kind of attitude or of mentality, a kind of tacit presupposition in regard to thought or action by men, which is never put in doubt by the social group concerned, but determines all their actions (cf. p. 1).

[33] Cf. *op. cit.*, p. 19.

[34] *Op. cit.*, p. 29.

[35] *Op. cit.*, p. 32.

[36] *Op. cit.*, p. 33.

"only this view of the confrontation that seems to me adequate for Marxism."[37]

But what is the outcome of this confrontation? It can be briefly summarized as follows: Greek myth showed a certain dualism; in the Judaic myth Gardavský finds a certain "monism", in the sense that it is "concerned with that relation between man and reality, by which man is not substantially divided from nature, or divided within himself ("dualized"). "We have thus a human condition which, in history, comes before the decisive step to the division of labour." "In this situation it is man who acts with his entire self . . . and what he does is play . . . not work; play, which is creativity."[38] However, "Biblical mythology, which here differs from Greek mythology, expresses the original human condition in which man's life, the life of the tribal community, was still play".[39] In this context God becomes "not a supernatural being of the same type as the gods on Olympus, a kind of personification of the forces of nature and mankind, given an anthropomorphic form, but rather an original way in which Judaic mythology gains consciousness of itself and gives expression to the dramatic quality of situations, in which the decision is taken about the direction in which history should proceed. Through the word and the name of God the Old Testament expresses everything that forms a part in the creative process, and that which induces this process. This is what causes the result to be highly unpredictable."[40]

In this way Gardavský finds in the true biblical tradition a third practical idea, "in which man finds his central interest in his power of deciding (given to him by nature)—of being creative".[41] According to Gardavský, this idea is also to be found in Marxism. This is why "the confrontation of Marxism with the Judaic idea is of equal importance to the traditional confrontation with the ancient classical world". For the same reason the dialogue with Christianity as the heir to and promoter of this idea is of vital importance to Marxism. The ideological struggle

[37] *Ibid.*
[38] *Op. cit.*, p. 52.
[39] *Op. cit.*, p. 54.
[40] *Op. cit.*, p. 40.
[41] *Op. cit.*, p. 64.

carried on by Marxism with Christianity should not be characterized by a narrow-minded mentality, since the question is not about belief and unbelief, but a principle which is found in both: for both practical ideas comprise a mutual exclusion of man and power.[42] Therefore Communists, according to the writer, should dissuade Christians from pursuing power-interests, and Communism "should give equal validity to non-power and power".[43] This would mean that Socialism, as it grows in maturity, should gradually give up power in favour of free decision.[44] This free renunciation of power by the Communist Party, foreshadowed and commended by Gardavský, gave an enthusiastic impetus to the "Prague Spring". A fact without precedent in history was brought to naught by a military intervention (but was it only by that intervention?). This is a proof that the power-interests are still stronger than the power of truly human interests.

In this way Gardavský's thinking develops from a confrontation of the Catholic argument with the Marxist argument, in the *Phenomenon Germania*, through an attempt at a deeper metaphysical analysis of Marxism in which the writer discovers that God is not wholly dead and ends, in his *The Sceptic's Hope*, with an interpretation of the "Judaic-Christian myth", which finds "a form of creativity" in the idea of God. This interpretation should lead, in the interests of the emancipation of human creativity, to a renunciation of power. This is the crowning thought of the Czech Marxist philosopher.

*Translated by Alec Randall*

[42] *Ibid.*
[43] *Op. cit.*, p. 65.
[44] *Op. cit.*, p. 66.

# Marc Alyn

# God in Contemporary Literature

IT IS above all in literature, the art of language, that the spiritual reveals itself. Through syllables the Absolute comes to us across immeasurable expanses of silence. Just as man belongs to the two kingdoms, here and beyond, the temporal and the eternal, so language is double. If one looks at it historically, it is a simple code, a currency of signs used by all the mouths in Babel, but at the other extreme it remains the Word which in the beginning produced the Light and still remembers it, as can be seen even now from images and rhythms which shine spontaneously, so it seems, at the four corners of language—and which we call poetry, for want of a less vague term.

By its unique situation at the intersection of the visible and the invisible, language reveals itself as the ideal conductor of the divine. A constant current of language connects heaven and earth. The prophets empty themselves for the invasion of the Word, which they then re-echo among men. Prayer, on the other hand, is the soul's word struggling to return to the creator of all language. Everything to do with language, beyond normal communication, can become the bearer—more often than not unconsciously—of signs indicating the progress (the degree of presence or absence) of God in the midst of us. From this point of view, literature at a certain elevation or depth takes on a value infinitely surpassing the categories of culture, information or entertainment; it becomes the creature's dialogue with its creator. The perspective is vast. Drop by drop, word by word, the soul filters humanity as a stalactite slowly grows through the millennia.

For a long time the shadow of God mingled on the page with that of man at the mercy of the word. The bent back of the scribe at work shows this pressure of the Spirit on the being in recollection. In the silence about the writer, words came into being. The visible and the invisible made two sides of a harmonious equilibrium. Day and night followed each other smoothly in a sequence as predictable as death replacing life, once the ellipse of personal destiny was complete. God was near, even for those who staked everything on earth, the flesh and the moment. In the West, Christianity gave daily life its energy and colour, from the humblest gestures to major acts. In the country the churches seemed to anchor the beyond on the surface of the real.

It is hard for us to imagine this sense of the closeness of the sacred, for the history of Western spirituality seems to be a gradual retreat of immediate, palpable signs of the divine. Through being purified, made to grow, to rid itself of its accumulation of superstitions and popular rites, the idea of God has become so intellectualized itself that it keeps a growing number of the faithful at a respectful distance. Through the complexity of his approach God became the concern of a few; through his cosmic dimensions he lost his familiar appearance—he moved away. "Heaven has moved away", Mallarmé was to say in a tone of solemn jubilation which, to all appearances, concealed a disappointed hope. Modern literature as a whole describes (explicitly or unconsciously) this epic in reverse: the withdrawal of God into infinity and the loneliness of humanity abandoned to the nothingness of objects.

The evolution in the idea of God corresponds to an upheaval in man and in the planet which supports him. The transition from an agricultural to an industrial society is such as to make a great difference to the perceptual structures of those who undergo it. After millennia of relative fixity man discovered speed (of action and movement) at the very moment when he was being caught up by it—a speed which transformed not only the appearance of countries but ideas. Can one make the same judgment of a place on a peaceful walk and from a fast car? The same applies to God seen by men caught up by a constant acceleration and without the time needed to readjust their metaphysical measuring systems.

The first symptoms of the absence or death of God appeared in the mid-nineteenth century, with the beginning of industrial civilization. Even though the most garrulous of the Romantics were carried away by optimism and saw the factory as the church of a new religion of progress, others prophesied the growing enslavement of man by the machine—which means, ultimately, by matter. Some even denounced as a lie (or at the very least an illusion) the claim that the machine would be able to give man more control over his most precious possession, his time. They saw the inevitable development of the modern economic system allowing no respite to the individual imprisoned in a production system that must constantly expand and in a consumption system artificially maintained by the creation of wants, by advertising. Material prosperity grows to staggering proportions, while anguish and a sense of emptiness spread among souls. The individual is at last able to affirm himself, but he no sooner does so than he is sucked back into the anonymity of the mass; this exerts such a pressure on him that in the end he has only the vaguest awareness of the shape of his own personality. And above all, there is never enough time. The machines and their products pursue a man into his spare time and his sleep. Now new gods arise, gleaming, strange, dumb, wearing plastic, painted metal chrome, nylon, synthetic leather: cold idols. Forced to live for things, man gradually becomes a sort of object.

Contrary to the widely held opinion, the terrifying philosophical hypothesis of the "death of God" derives not from Nietzsche but from the German Romantic Jean Paul. His "Dream", written in 1790, paints a frightening picture of a creation deprived of its creator: "Wherever you go, sun, with your planets, in the whole of your course you will find no trace of God . . . of the God who was painted as a glittering eye there is now nothing left but a black gaping socket. . . ." Jean Paul remarked later, "The first conception of this piece was terrifying to my soul, and I trembled as I wrote it."

The poem had a considerable influence on the French Romantics, and Gérard de Nerval took from it the idea of his *Christ aux Oliviers,* which has the following two lines of Jean Paul's as an epigraph:

> Dieu est mort! Le ciel est vide...
> Pleurez, enfants, vous n'avez plus de père!

Nerval's poem presents a Christ desperate and abandoned crying to his "unfaithful friends":

> Frères, je vous trompais: Abîme, abîme, abîme!
> Le dieu manque à l'autel où je suis la victime...
> Dieu n'est pas! Dieu n'est plus!—Mais ils dormaient
>                                          toujours....

Vigny was to write *Le Mont des Oliviers* on the same subject, but here the existence of God is not questioned; the subject is silence and distance:

> Mais le ciel reste noir et Dieu ne répond pas.

*Le silence* is the title of a text by Vigny which continues the previous one and gives it a Stoic ending:

> Le juste opposera le dédain à l'absence
> Et ne répondra plus que par un froid silence
> Au silence éternel de la Divinité.

The circle is thus complete. The modern vocabulary of dereliction ("absence", "silence", "death") had already been created in its entirety in the nineteenth century. From now on we shall meet these words at every step.

It would nevertheless be a mistake to think that literature did no more than acknowledge the withdrawal or disappearance of the sacred. From Rimbaud to Gerard Manley Hopkins, on the contrary, the spiritual search often took the form of a confrontation between the soul and its God, who seemed to retreat. The allegory of Jacob wrestling with the angel was from this point of view a perfect description of the interior adventure of many poets in the last century. What else did these "terrible workers" of Rimbaud's want than to pierce the layers of steel, concrete and cynicism which had made a wall between the creature and the absolute? Even the search for a hell ("Hell", said Barbey d'Aurevilly, "is the image of heaven reversed") carried out by means of clairvoyance, eroticism ("a disturbance of all the senses") or the "artificial paradises" of drugs is evidence of a thwarted striving towards another world which will not approach us.

Ungaretti has described very well this presence of the divine in authors who themselves deny it: "There is nevertheless in these modern poems . . . an apprehension of the sacred with an effect on the poetry which grows stronger the more the poem thinks itself distant from the divine."

One thing is certain. With a few exceptions (the softness of Rilke or Milosz, the inspired violence of Claudel) spiritual scenery as writers describe it is negative: a gloomy, painful desert. Even though the surrealists found hope in social revolution, psycho-analysis or magic, they helped to plant man even more firmly in the world of matter by including in the material the unconscious, chance and dreams. For André Breton "the beyond, the whole of the beyond, is in this life", which in the end simply makes the "surreal" a higher degree in the scale of reality which, since it does not lead to God, leads nowhere.

At the other extreme from surrealism, Paul Valéry refused even to dream. He was not excited by chimeras, and regarded God as a problem in the mathematical sense. He complained that Pascal had wasted his time defending and explaining re-ligion when he might have developed algebra. Valéry's experi-ence in his famous "nuit de Gênes" was almost the reverse of Pascal's illumination: a "mystical" experience in reverse which revealed to him the primacy of nothingness in the universe. It is clear how far we have travelled since Mallarmé trembled as he described "ce vieux méchant plumage enfin terrassé, Dieu". There is no struggle with the angel for Valéry, who limits him-self to noting that the angel does not exist and that any action would be useless.

Sartre's existentialism starts even more clearly from a profes-sion of faith—so to speak—in atheism. Only the requirements of the theatre made Sartre create the tyrannical figure of Jupiter in *The Flies* and to take up, in *Le Diable et le Bon Dieu*, Jean Paul's and Nietzsche's cry: "God is dead. . . . I tell you God is dead!" These are dramatized ideas, serving the purposes of a trial decided in advance. Sartre never seriously envisaged the dis-appearance of a God who, in his view, never existed except in man's timid imagination. So when Crestes pours out his famous tirade, "Jupiter, you are the king of the gods, the king of stones and stars, the king of the waves of the sea. But you are not the king of men", it is clear that we are listening to a flight of rhetoric much more than a real statement. Sartre's fictitious divinity enjoyed no "kingship", not even over stars, seasons or objects.

Less complex and more "sensitive" is the attitude of Camus, who also rejects God in favour of man, but from a moral rather than a philosophical standpoint. "I will die rather than love a creation in which children are tortured." Evil, in Camus's work, is regarded exclusively as God's doing, in a slightly facile dialectic which may be summarized as follows: If God exists he is all-powerful; suffering and evil pursue the innocent, the "just", across the face of the earth; therefore, evil is the work of God, simply by the fact of his permitting it. There is certainly more generosity, but less logic, in this attitude than in Sartre's. Sartre offers man revolution in exchange for the grace of which he deprives him, while Camus offers him only revolt, which is little more than the individual consciousness' gesture of indignation, an ineffectual attitude. As a man of the golden mean, Camus never made a total choice; he puts his money on the earth, but without illusions, though at the same time he creates in Caligula a thirst for "something which might be made, but would not be of this world". In terms of modern politics, this attitude would be called "centrism".

One of the most representative products of the spiritual crisis of the twentieth century is the mysterious work of Kafka. Has the world suddenly begun to resemble Kafka's visions, or was Kafka a prophet, living through in advance on the level of ideas and feelings the grim developments of future history? No one knows, since Kafka never compared himself with any writer of the past or present. From his childhood Kafka was alone, deprived of all contact with the members of his family, incapable of communicating. The words at his disposal are no use as elements of a dialogue: they would not be understood. He must drive them back until they can be committed to paper and ink. If Kafka remains silent, shut up in himself as in a fortress-prison, it is because he can offer no more than negative words, which would drive mad those who, absurdly, are said to be close to him. He has recognized himself definitively as a secret traveller in a universe in which appearances are the supreme values, to be saved at all costs if the mechanisms of existence are not to be destroyed. "If I begin physically to resemble my ideas", he thinks, "those who say they love me will be horrified; they will reject me in terror. What can this 'love' be that stops at the first obstacle and changes into hatred when a few scales and feelers appear at the edges of this perishable flesh?"

As a result of this experience, Kafka went on to examine the spectacle of humanity enslaved to appearances, and brought to this examination a purity of vision. He saw a chaos of gestures, leaps towards nothing, a series of interlocking solitudes trying vainly to connect in order to do away with fear, the true condition of the creature, the only fixed point on that living wheel which crushes others and then shatters itself.

An order can nevertheless be discerned in this absurdity. There must be someone at a distance supervising the application of the penalty to which men have been condemned. And surely this condemnation must be the result of a Judgment? If that is so, then somewhere there must be a Tribunal, a written Law, counsel and—who knows?—possibilities of appeal, reduction of sentence, pardon. After all, it would not be logical to imagine that everyone could have been sent to the same "penal colony" for a collective Fault and almost forgotten. There is no time to waste; one must begin to look for the invisible Tribunal which will decide. The soul appeals for the reopening of its "case". But the judge is inaccessible, buried far away in the depths of the labyrinth of corridors, halls, offices, cells which makes up the Tribunal. As "untouchable" as the Emperor in the story of *The Great Wall of China*, whose message indeed really leaves the palace on its way to each of his subjects, but has to cover so much ground on its way that the addressee will probably die without receiving the letter. . . .

It can be seen that the "death of God" in Kafka is certainly not taken for granted; this removes the character of absolute despair which has too readily been ascribed to his work. True, no one has seen the Judge or Emperor with physical eyes, but one does have a sense of his presence, formidable, eternal, in a remote region of infinity. Nor is God silent; he has simply moved so far from humanity that when his word reaches them it is inevitably distorted by the considerable length of time needed for his Voice to travel through space. Absolute beauty—which is justice—remains accessible to the creature who suffers and waits without tiring: "If it is summoned by the right word, by its real name, it comes."

One might explore this central problem further by examining the meaning of *"waiting"* for Beckett (Godot, after all, is God, as his name suggests), or of *"proliferation"* (the words, the rhinoceroses and the corpse which grows in *How to Get Rid of It*) for Ionesco. Similarly, an analysis of current poetic language would show the obsession with absence, silence, and blank pages and the curious desire to limit the word to its material components. What remedy can be used to treat this cancer of the spirit which is gnawing at our age? T. S. Eliot has told us: "The world is in the process of trying to construct a non-Christian mentality. The experiment will fail, but we must show a great deal of patience in waiting for that failure, and we must still redeem the time: in order to keep the faith alive during the coming dark ages; in order to renew and rebuild civilization; in order to save the world from suicide."

*Translated by Francis McDonagh*

Jacques Kamstra

# Changes in the Idea of God in Non-Western Religions and Cultures

WE IN the West pay more attention to the problem of God in the non-Western religions and cultures than the members of those religions. Furthermore, we have often tended to approach this problem with a certain feeling of superiority, both in the case of cultures without a written literature and in the case of universal religions such as Buddhism. Societies without a written religious tradition have been regarded as possessing only a minimal idea of God. In some cases, there is just a belief in souls and spirits, totems and forces. In others, there is a belief in demons and gods and in many cases a debased monotheism, sometimes approaching our own.

What has almost always remained obscure, however, is the precise way in which the idea of God was experienced. Almost always, any change in the idea of God held by peoples without a written culture has been approached from a Western point of view. We are less inclined nowadays to force the religious convictions of such peoples as the Bantu, pygmies, Indians and others into a preconceived pattern, and are more anxious to see them as they really are. We tend to be on our guard against speaking about the sacred element as power and will, as G. van der Leeuw[1] did in the nineteen-fifties, because that sacred element hardly exists as an impersonal power. To give one example —the Melanesian word *mana* emphasizes a relationship with a personal spiritual being and, despite what Durkheim and van der

[1] G. van der Leeuw, *Phänomenologie der Religion* (Tübingen, 1956), pp. 83 ff.

Leeuw say, cannot be used to designate an impersonal concept of God. We can only conclude that every group's concept of God is quite unique, with the result that comparative religion is a very difficult discipline indeed.

Nor is it any easier to classify the sacred element in such universal religions as Buddhism and Hinduism in our Western concepts. Very little help is afforded by using a system of antitheses such as monotheism-pantheism (or monism), transcendence-immanence or theism-atheism. These and similar contrasts, so common in Western thinking, bring us no closer to an understanding of the universal religions of the East. They too have forms of monotheism and are open to the idea of divine transcendence. We in the West tend to call Buddhism essentially atheistic, but this is almost entirely the result of faulty observation on our part. Buddha did not speak of the sacred element, but this was not because he did not recognize its existence, but because he spoke above all in accordance with the idea of God prevalent at his time, which he left unchanged, and also because he believed that this was a reality about which the unenlightened man *could not* say anything. His attitude, then, was not so atheistic as that of our "God is dead" theologians. Our theological concepts cannot be applied to other world religions until their meaning is made perfectly clear.

Contact with the West has undoubtedly led to changes in the idea that such peoples have of God. I should therefore like to consider four types of non-Western religion for the purpose of showing how, in one type, the whole society can lead to a new concept of God and, in another, this is brought about by certain religious factors. The four types of religion are tribal religions, national religions, universal religions, the personal religions.

## I. Tribal Religions

Barrett[2] has described a tribe as a collection or group of people with a common name, language, culture and territory, with a tradition of common descent, an ideological unity and a consciousness of belonging together. The collectivity of the group is more important than each individual. The concept of God in

[2] D. B. Barrett, *Schism and Renewal in Africa* (Nairobi, 1968), p. 44.

such a group plays an important part in its conviction of common descent and in its ideology. One very important factor to bear in mind in considering tribal religion is its magnitude and diversity—it has been suggested that there are more than one hundred thousand tribes living south of the Sahara alone.

Early theories about animistic, totemistic and primitive monotheistic religions have been disproved by recent research into these religions, which has shown how varied the tribal gods and their attributes can be. Many, for example, are both one and yet pluriform, spiritual and yet visible in many different symbols. The god Kwoth of the Nuer tribe in Eastern Sudan, for example, is the spirit of heaven where he lives, is invisible as the air and omnipresent as the universe. At the same time, however, he reveals himself in the wind and the rain and shines in the sun and the moon. The spirits in heaven are also regarded as "Kwoth going", that is, as the children of Kwoth. Some birds, at least the high-flying birds, are also called "Kwoth going".

The god Wakan Tanka of the Oglala Indians has been provided with a scheme by the shamans of the tribe, showing that he embodies a number of other tribal gods and spirits in himself:

| sun | | |
|-----|---|---|
| moon | | |
| buffalo | head god | |
| spirit | | Wakan Tanka |
| heaven | | |
| wind | great spirit | |
| bear | | |
| spirit | | |

This example and others like it[3] show that no clear distinction can be made even at this stage between monotheism and polytheism. Even the gods of the primitive peoples cannot be easily categorized and put into a neat scientific pigeon-hole. The only statement that can be made categorically about all tribal gods is that they are limited to the territory occupied by the tribe. Kwoth of the Nuer is only a god where the Nuer are. In exchange for the territorial and tribal limitations imposed on him,

[3] T. P. van Baaren, "Pluriform Monotheism", *Nederlands Theologisch Tijdschrift*, 20 (1966), pp. 312-27.

he controls all spheres of life, including the economic and political spheres, of the Nuer tribe. Nadel[4] has said of the Nupe that the totality of beliefs and practices, known as Nupe, Yoruba or Gwari religion, is simply the religion of those people who, for other reasons, call themselves Nupe, Yoruba or Gwari. He says that it may be possible for individual customs or even matters of belief to be accepted or borrowed, but that to export the religion as a whole or to exchange it for another would be unthinkable. The Nupe are very willing to talk with their neighbours about *their* religions, and even approve of those religions, however different they may be from their own. But, because they are Nupe, they keep to their own religion. In these and other tribal religions, the existence of the deity stands or falls with the existence of the tribe.

Changes in tribal life are almost always accompanied by changes in the tribal religion and it is possible to distinguish movements in two directions in this phenomenon. The first of these tendencies, which is taking place currently in many sects in Africa, has the form of an attempt to change the Christian or Muslim concept of God into the idea of God prevalent in the tribe, an attempt to make the universal God into a purely local god. The claim of Kimbangism in the Congo, for example, is that God is—not exclusively, it is true—the God of Africa.

Many African prophets see God as he was seen by the Jewish people in the Old Testament, and African leaders such as Hendrik Witbooi are seen as fulfilling the same function as Moses leading his people to freedom. Others are prepared to accept a Christian God, but not without an earthly goddess—this is apparently the case among 31% of African tribes. Even those who accept a biblical concept of God find it impossible to give up their own tribal ancestors, whom they regard as divine and as ultimately responsible for all good and evil, health, growth and strength. This accounts for the characteristic name "Church of Our Ancestors" (with variants) for so many independent sects in Kenya, Malawi, South Congo and elsewhere. The Lord's Supper is combined with special services for ancestors in the Herero Church of South-West Africa. The angel's reproach that the

[4] S. F. Nadel, *Nupe Religion* (London, 1954), p. 227.

spirits of the ancestors are neglected is often heard in the Zionist churches of the Zulus. The cargo cults of New Guinea provide an interesting variant of this ancestor worship, even Christians leaving their churches at certain times because they too are convinced that their ancestors will come with ships laden with Western cargo. Perhaps the most striking aspect of this tendency in sects everywhere is that more emphasis is placed on the role of the prophet, the redeemer, the healer or the Messiah than on any revolutionary idea of God.

The second of these tendencies is that contact with the Christian civilization of the West has meant, in many cases, that the tribal gods have simply ceased to exist. To give a concrete example, fetishism has been done away with in Congolese Kimbangism. It is, however, beyond the scope of this article to examine the extent to which this elimination of tribal gods has resulted in a change in the concept of God.

## II. The National Religions

In this type of religion, several tribes live in the territory of one deity as a political unit or nation. What often happens is that the god of one particular tribe becomes a national deity to which the other neighbouring tribes are subjected, and who speaks through the political leaders of the superior tribe, who are usually more important than the god himself. The nation is given its national status by its god in very much the same way as the tribe receives its status from the tribal god.

I should like to consider only one of the many examples of this national type of religion—Shintoism in Japan, which originated as a combination of the many gods of ancient Japan in a family tree which showed them all to be members of the one family. Although this combination was achieved some one thousand three hundred years ago, it has never been entirely satisfactory. Just before the Second World War, Shintoism was used to stimulate Japanese nationalism, a central part being played in this whole complex by the Emperor as a deity descended from the chief goddess Amaterasu. Japan is the land of eight million *kami* who were gods in a very special way, closely related to the characteristic form of Japanese religiosity. This has been described by E. Pirijns[5] as moving "in a cosmic dimension and direction, in which the Absolute is rooted in the phenomenal and the intramundane".

Comparing the religion of Japan with that of China, the Japanese author Fujitani[6] has said that, whereas the Chinese thought of heaven as spiritual, the Japanese saw it simply as the visible firmament. The gods descended from heaven to earth and maintained contact with heaven. One of these deities was the ancestor of the Emperor, although not only his, but the ancestors of other ancient clans came down from heaven. In the eighth century, Fujitani tells us, Amaterasu, the Emperor's ancestor, came to represent national unity and the ideal of imperial rule. In ancient Japan, moreover, there were no symbols for the deities —the mountain itself, a river, a wood, a tree, an animal, a stone, the sun, the rain and the wind were all gods. The gods of Shinto were therefore a part of everyday human life—as long as he lived, man was surrounded by these gods; when he died, however, he went to an invisible heaven. What is particularly interesting in this connection is that this heaven does not belong to Shintoism, but to Buddhism, which waits for the Japanese believer in heaven with sacred figures such as the Buddha of the future Maitreya or the merciful Lord Amitābha. There is no competition between Shintoism and Buddhism in the life of the Japanese believer— each has its own special sphere.

The failure of this Shinto concept of God was made public on 1 January 1946 in a broadcast by Emperor Hirohito,[7] in which he declared that the bonds between the Japanese nation and himself were based on mutual trust and love and not on myths and legends. They were not, he insisted, based on the false idea that the Emperor was divine and that the Japanese nation was superior to other nations and predestined to rule the world. Of course, Hirohito voluntarily said this at the suggestion of his American advisers, but it administered a fatal blow to the Shinto concept of God. If the Emperor was no longer a deity, a great number of other *kami* lost their divinity. The divine lineage of the Emperor

---

[5] E. Pirijns, *Japan en het Christendom*, Vol. I (Lannoo, 1971), p. 264.

[6] Saki Akio *et al.*, *Gendai Nihon Shukyō-hihan* (Tokyo, 1967), p. 198.

[7] W. H. M. Creemers, *Shrine Shinto after World War II* (Leiden, 1968), p. 227.

was gone, together with the originator of that line, Amaterasu, and indeed all the other divine ancestors of the Japanese nation. Since the Second World War, Shintoism has become, for most Japanese people, little more than an interesting aspect of folk-lore. Fernando M. Basabe has reported that at least 82% of the male population in the towns between the ages of twenty and forty no longer believe in it.[8]

For some time before the Emperor's declaration of 1946, doubts as to whether the *kami* were really divine had existed because the manipulations of the Shinto concept of God in order to further nationalism had been obvious to many people in Japan. These doubts led to a development in the opposite direction, and there was a complete break with the nationalistic concept of God in certain renewal movements which had taken Shintoism as their point of departure. The prevalent concept of God in these re-newal movements, the best known of which is Tenrikyō, is similar to that of the universal religions. Three different ex-amples may help to illustrate this.[9]

The Ōmotokyō movement was founded in 1892 by a deeply concerned housewife, Nao Deguchi, and flourished in the years preceding the Second World War, when there were some two million members led by Nao Deguchi's companion, Onisaburō, named by the foundress as the saviour of the world. Since the War, this group has attempted to fill the gap left empty by the failure of Shinto, claiming that "our environment is filled with God, Buddha or Maitreya—man and God must become one". In this declaration, the word *kami* is used for God, but according to a new etymological derivation, *kami* is believed to have come from *kakuremi*, "hidden body", and, by using this derivation, the movement attempts to dissociate itself from *kami* in the traditional sense.

The Konkōkyō, founded in 1859, has expressed its extreme dis-approval of traditional Shintoism by elevating *kane no kami*, the "iron god", an evil spirit causing wilting and death in Shinto, to the status of the god of heaven and earth, father of the universe and of all mankind and patron of all welfare in heaven and on

[8] Fernando M. Basabe, *Religious Attitudes of Japanese Men* (Tokyo, 1968), pp. 23, 109.
[9] H. Thomsen, *The New Religions of Japan* (Rutland, Vermont, 1963).

earth. This is, of course, a protest against the Shinto establishment.

The Kuromizukyō was founded by Kuromizu, who raised Amaterasu to the level of a monotheistic god "who crowns the universe with the glory of the teaching" of the Kuromizukyō. The relationship between Amaterasu and the other eight million gods is expressed thus: "The one God is embodied in a million gods and a million gods are found in the one God; everything is attributed to the one God."

It is clear, then, that the defeat of nationalism can lead either to the total disappearance of purely national religions or to a widening of their perspectives to the extent that they become universal.

### III. THE UNIVERSAL RELIGIONS

By a "universal religion" is meant a religion whose membership is not to be determined by membership of a tribe or a nation, but by personal choice. The founder of a universal religion makes an appeal to every man as a human being, thus transcending the boundaries imposed by tribe, nation or territory. The concept of God current in universal religions is not territorially limited, but expresses a relationship between God and the whole of mankind. The world may be created by God, as the Christians, Jews and Muslims believe, or it may be an outward manifestation of the deity, as the Hindus and Buddhists believe.

As I pointed out at the beginning of this article, we have to be very careful when considering this contrast between these two groups of universal religions. In the case of Christianity, Judaism and Islam, God is the ultimate principle. Although some Buddhist groups do in fact use the name of God in principle, this is not the case in Buddhism as a whole. The only affirmation made by Japanese Buddhists, for example, is that every man has in his possession the initial means of reaching the ultimate goal, the nature of Buddha.

To reconcile these two contrasting groups of world religions is a difficult task. If any change takes place in their concept of God, this is to a very great extent discernible at the point where they meet and are separated. Apart from India, where movements in this direction are certainly taking place, there have, since the War, been very great changes in the Buddhist concept of God in Japan. The Sokagakkai movement, which has increased its membership in nineteen years from three thousand to fifteen million, is a striking example of this. In 1966, its leader, Ikeda, wrote, in a rather apologetic, yet aggressive article,[10] that Christians in worshipping God and Muslims in worshipping Allah were only venerating illusions—they were ignorant of the existence of the true Buddha. What mankind was seeking was nothing but the true Buddha. Even when a man prayed to God, Ikeda insisted, he could not become a god. But, in praying to the true Buddha and calling upon the holy title of Buddha, he can obtain the same enlightenment and reach the same state as the true Buddha. It is fairly clear from these words that the idea of God has been changed by the Sokagakkai movement in the same way as it was changed by the Japanese Buddhists more than eleven hundred years ago from the concept of *kami*. For the Sokagakkai, God is the imperfect manifestation of the eternal and invisible nature of Buddha.

Less aggressive and more irenic in its tone is the Seicho-no-Ie, the "House of Adulthood", with more than six million members. This movement claims to transcend all denominations, teaching the truth that all religions come from a universal God. It is clearly a Japanese counterpart of the Sufi movement in Islam. When children are made members of the "Son of God Society" set up by this movement, they say: "I am a son of God. I am a son of Buddha. I can therefore do anything." The founder of the movement, Masaharu Taniguchi, has said that the Seicho-no-Ie is the "means of perfecting the indwelling God and the nature of Buddha through the creative power of the word".[11]

These two statements show that both the Sokagakkai and the Seicho-no-Ie have done no more than juxtapose two different ideas of God and thus pose the problem again without offering any real solution. The situation is very similar in the case of most other Japanese religious groups of a universal nature.

[10] See *Nichiren Shoshu Sokagakkai* (Tokyo, 1966), p. 188.
[11] Taken from a pamphlet published in November 1962 by the Seicho-no-Ie.

I briefly alluded to India at the beginning of this section. Despite the fact that the history of Hinduism is a history of uninterrupted integration, there are no great movements in India, like those in Japan, which aim to integrate their concept of God with those of other universal religions. Any extensions of the Hindu concept of God are almost exclusively done with apologetic aims in mind. Two examples which spring to mind are the writings of Radhakrishnan, for example,[12] on the one hand, and those of Zaehner[13] on the other. Simplifying the situation radically, one might say that the Indian author's aim is to subordinate Christianity to Hinduism, whereas the Western writer, despite his excellence, is attempting to present Christianity as the fulfilment of Hinduism. As Klostermaier has correctly observed,[14] the only purpose served by such attempts is to convince those who are already convinced of the truth of their own faith. We may in any case conclude by saying that we are still at the beginning stages of this integration, at a point where it is difficult to tell whether it is a religious task or a world-wide necessity.

## IV. INDIVIDUAL RELIGIONS

This is the type of religion favoured by the intellectual believer —usually a city-dweller—who for one reason or another rejects the other types outlined above. I have myself carried out a very limited sociological survey in this field, but much more extended research is required before the concepts that such people have of God can be fully known. From my own investigations, I have discovered that a whole scale of religions, belonging to all of three above-mentioned types, is to be found among such individual, independent believers, with the result that we may safely say that all the world religions are present in one form or another in our world centres, such as Amsterdam, New York or Tokyo. It may also be that there is more totemism and dynamism among such people than among primitive people.

---

[12] See, e.g., Radhakrishnan, *Religion in a Changing World* (London, 1967).

[13] See, e.g., R. C. Zaehner, *Concordant Discord* (Oxford, 1970).

[14] K. Klostermaier, *Hinduismus* (Cologne, 1965), pp. 406, 405.

## V. Conclusion

Clearly changes are taking place everywhere in the concept of God. Basically, these changes are in two directions—from the tribal to the individual or personal concept and, above all, from the individual to the tribal concept of God. The static concept of God familiar to specialists in comparative religion in the past has now become dynamic. But it is not characterized by a movement towards Christianity—in Japan alone, both Buddhism and Christianity seem to be on the decline. None the less, it is a fascinating experience to be living at a time when everyone seems to be more than ever looking for the true God.

*Translated by David Smith*

Guy Deleury

# A Hindu God for Technopolis?

THE history of civilizations is the history of their deicides. Ever since his unknown beginnings, man has massacred gods on an incredible scale. Judaism, Christianity and Islam cheerfully destroyed "false gods", Zoroastrianism made them angels, Hinduism made them a low caste (if not untouchables), and Buddhism played with them like a king with his fools. Europe, now Christian, in its turn unleashed a general offensive which left the niches of its cathedrals bare and desecrated the altars. The man of technopolis at the dawn of the new civilization produced by his brain and his machines finds himself suddenly attacked by loneliness and looks desperately for the new face of this God who refuses to die.

There is a rumour that God is still alive in the land of India. The new pilgrims, guitars on their shoulders and marihuana in their pockets, flock in their thousands towards the Himalayas without ski-lifts, the wild Ganges, unpolluted beaches. Katmandu, Benares and Goa are the new Jerusalems. Ashrams turn people away, and amazed gurus distribute initiations to these strange, fair-skinned disciples.

Meanwhile young Indians crowd the airports to seek in the West the secrets of this paradise from which the gods who still keep them in slavery have been driven out.

The theologian watching the exodus and the arrival of the newcomers is faced with the question: Who is this God who attracts by his mystery and repels when familiar? We must start by admitting that language fails us; there is no Sanskrit word to translate "God", just as there is no English word for "Brahman". Nevertheless we must try to give an answer, and this article must use inadequate translations: for "Brahman", "Hindu God" (though there are many more), and "Christian God" for the God whose death has recently been celebrated by the theologians. Our investigation starts from an actual situation; having killed their God, young Westerners from the Christian tradition expect to find an answer to their spiritual quest in the Hindu God from whom the young Hindus are trying to free themselves.

The young people are in the process of discovering, with their feet, the *whole* earth. Let us confess that it is the revolution in communications which has stimulated our present reflections— we were happy in our ghettos. Every religion thought of itself as a totality, in superb ignorance of the "heathen", "kaffirs" or "mlecchas" who persisted in living beyond its cultural frontiers. It took the Churches nineteen centuries and twenty-one allegedly "ecumenical" Councils to recognize the right of Hindus and other "non-Christians" to religious existence. Young people are born into an already pluralist world in which no one would dream of asking the classic question, "How could anyone be a Persian?" Justly unjust, they attack the theologian: "Why did you hide from us for so long the riches which are ours by right of universal inheritance?" Jesus enters into competition with Krishna on a now international market.

Christians made this geographical myopia worse with their own particular historical spectacles. Only recently a good theologian could write: "The true relation between Christianity and all other religions is the following: they all come *before* it, they have all been overtaken. I do not say that they are completely false; Judaism, Buddhism and the fetishist civilizations are not in the first place false but old; that is to say, they belong to the time *before* Christianity and are as it were survivals."[1] Today's generation is discovering that the reality is different. Hinduism is still young, and it is the Christian God who seems to them obsolete. Robinson rejects the traditional conception of the Judaeo-Christian personal God in favour of a God curiously similar to

[1] J. Daniélou, *The Advent of Salvation* (Glen Rock, 1962), p. 18.

the Hindu God, and (according to Robinson) more in harmony with modern civilization.[2]

But who is this "Hindu God"? Is he what the modern West has been looking for? What question does he pose for the "Christian God?"

## The Migratory Bird

> The Migratory bird
> enters into every creature
> and becomes present in them
> like fire in sticks rubbed together:
> Knowing this is to conquer death."
>
> (*Hamsa Upanishad*)[3]

The Brahman, in R. C. Zaehner's words, is "the impersonal principle of all being".[4] It does not act, it exists. When Yahweh reveals his name to Moses he explains immediately that it was He who brought Moses out of the land of Egypt. The Semitic God proves his existence by an action: Brahman does not need to prove his—he is existence. The whole of the Hindu religious attitude involves man's passing into existence, as this prayer from the Upanishads asks:

> "From the unreal lead me to the real!
> From darkness lead me to light.
> From death lead me to immortality."[5]

Man realizes himself by a long journey with various stages through successive unrealities; at the end of the process the individual soul (*atman*) discovers its fundamental identity with the universal soul (*brahman*); the migratory bird begins its motionless flight.

The Hindu God is the God the mystic discovers as he progresses in spirituality. He can be found in experience, but he is also incommunicable. Each person must have the experience for himself. Existence cannot be talked about, it has to be lived. The Hindu God is not the "totally other" but the ultimate self

[2] J. A. T. Robinson, *Honest to God* (London & New York, 1963), pp. 45–64.
[3] J. Varenne, *Upanishads du Yoga* (Paris, 1971), p. 111.
[4] R. C. Zaehner, *Hinduism* (London & New York, 1962), pp. 47–74.
[5] R. E. Hume, *The Thirteen Principal Upanishads* (London & New York, 1921), p. 80.

(*paramatman*). Certainly Hindu religious experience is not limited to mystical experience, but in the last analysis it is this experience which gives value to all the others.

Is this *brahman* the God young Westerners are looking for in their disillusionment with Christ and his Churches? It might seem so at first, since he is different from both the Christian God and the Marxist anti-God in the sense that he has no interest in history. For the Hindu, history has no meaning, or at most is a slide into chaos. The actual experience of man in the world is of a mad society in which insatiable desires produce suffering and death. In order to reach joy one must renounce the whole system (*sansara*).

The renunciation of the *sannyasi* is in many ways similar to that of the hippies; it includes renunciation of the social system, the family, comfort and conformity. It means physical departure from civilization, away from cities; wearing particular clothes or no clothes as a sign of one's liberation, long hair, unkempt beards or shaven heads; begging, and eating only foods which one thinks will not weigh down meditation or hinder the flight of the migratory bird. It involves continence or sexual licence according to need, the use of drugs or yoga techniques which facilitate forgetfulness of the body and the explosion of the real self; a search for the guru who will help one to recognize the stages and pass through them. This description of the *sannyasi* also fits the hippy.

The Hindu God promises absolute joy and peace in this life— not in an eschatological future but in this present life. He makes the body a necessary instrument of liberation, and rejects the Christian dichotomy of body and soul in which the search for God is called the "spiritual life"—an expression a Hindu finds absurd.

The final experience of *brahman* in *samadhi* is beyond any possible conceptualization, for the knower, the known and the act of knowing become identical in the experience of absolute existence. *Aham brahman*, "I am God", is the mystic's last word. The real man surpasses the actual man infinitely, just as *purusha* surpasses the phenomenal world. One day, the Semitic God promised, you will be as gods; in India, today. There man has conquered the tree of life by his techniques of renunciation and concentration; he is God. The fixed smile of the Buddha or of

Shiva the *mahayogi*, the naked body of Tirthankar Jain, express this state of divinity in which man, perfect at last, has suppressed the influences of space and time: the saint (*sant*) is the man who is (*sat*).

## The Brahman or the Cow

"To save a cow or a brahman
he must lay down his life without a second thought"
(*Manou*)[6]

There remain the men who do not "exist". The God we called at the beginning the Hindu God is the God of the *sannyasi*, of the man who has given up the world and, looking over his shoulder, as it were, gives the world he has left the positive value of unreality. He is the God of the man of leisure. Practising yoga or any other form of concentration demands a measure of time to spare and freedom from other concerns. The leisure itself is not of course the pleasure in this—far from it; giving up the world and mastering one's body is a sport reserved to a few champions. Society also must agree to maintain these unproductive members. The Hindu God thus turns out to be the God of a tiny élite concentrating in itself the perfection of humanity. *Brahman* is the God of the *brahman* (the highest caste), who is guaranteed a privileged existence by the work of the other castes. If the *brahman*'s duty (*dharma*) is to become a perfect man, that of the other castes is to give him alms. The huge mass of non-*brahmans* can only have a second-hand experience of the *brahman*'s God.

We now have, though as something of a paradox, the first part of the answer to our question. The Hindu God is the object of the present religious search in the West because the Westerner has become, on the world scale, the *brahman* of the world. The complementarity of developed country and developing country, West and Third World, corresponds in many respects to the opposition *brahman* and non-*brahman* in Hindu society. The Westerner, like the *brahman*, is born into privilege and the Indian is born into dependence on the privileged. The parallelism could be

[6] A. Loiseleur-Deslongchamps, *Lois de Manou* (Paris, 1939), XI, 79, p. 330.

taken even further: just as within the *brahman* caste there is a hierarchy of states of life (*ashramas*): the student, the father of a family, the recluse and the man who gives up everything, similarly in the West there is a whole class which opposes (gives up) the social order. The difference, symptomatic, as we shall see, is that in the Hindu structure, *sannyasya* (the state of being a *sannyasi*) is the final state of man, the end of the passage through the social order, both outside it and legitimating it, whereas being a hippy takes place before involvement in the society of producers.

Neither group can survive without a society to support it. The Hindu God is very much the God of the young protesters in that he is the God of the privileged. In the West many adults accuse the young of hypocrisy, but who in fact are the hypocrites if not they, living at the expense of the rest of the world, the *brahmanas* of the international caste system? The *brahman*, Hindu or Western, enjoys a certain security; he is at the top of the hierarchy, he cannot go any higher.[7] Because he is the principal beneficiary of the system he is also its most depersonalized member; more than anyone else he depends on the "system" from which he profits to the maximum.

The attitude of the average Western tourist visiting an under-developed country is typically "brahmanic". Without his gadgets, he lives in permanent fear of catching some outlandish disease; without realizing it, he treats the "natives" in the same way as the Hindu *brahman* treats the untouchables. His God is the one who maintains the established order but reduces him to the state of being a (happy) cog in a machine (*sansara*) which is hell for everyone else. The God of the hippy is the exact opposite; he promises individual liberation and gives absolute value to the "I".[8] He recognizes society's right to exist (the hippy is not a revolutionary), but claims for himself the right to leave it. He takes no interest in society.

There are also signposts along the path from the unreal to the real. The relation between the *sannyasi* en route and his God is experimental and not sacramental. The liturgical reform has hardly any chance of bringing our young pilgrims of the absolute

[7] L. Dumont, *Homo Hierarchicus* (Paris, 1966), pp. 324–50.
[8] L. D. Streiker, *The Gospel of Irreligious Religion* (New York, 1969), p. 77.

back to the Churches.[9] It is the sacramental system itself which they regard as questionable and outdated. The Hindu God they see over the head of the Christian God does not ask them to believe but to feel. They do not look for their salvation to an invisible power outside themselves but to a gradual liberation earned by hard work on their body and their selves. Some of them hope to find a short cut through the use of drugs, but this does not alter the fact that the basic desire of the "affluent" young is to devote their whole being to finding the absolute. The God of the *sannyasi* seems to fit this desire.

But what is the cost? The existence of the *brahman* is inextricably linked with that of his cow; in other words, with caste society. Through his mystical experience, the man who gives up society gives society the God who is its basis, even if in order to find him he has to leave society while continuing a liberated life within it. India loves those of her people who give up society, because she knows that without them she would die of emptiness.

Finally, therefore, the Hindu God appears as something different from the hippy's goal, whatever he may believe. The Hindu God cannot exist outside a village society divided into castes. He is in some way pre-industrial. When young people look beyond their own frontiers in space they are really looking back in time.

### The "Third Man"

"I felt that I had at last discovered by religion, the religion of man." (Tagore)[10]

The closer the hippy God comes to the Hindu God, the further he goes from the unknown God sought in the darkness by a man from a neon-lit civilization, who finds his liberation in anonymity and mobility.[11] This mobility, but not the anonymity, is a true sannyasic virtue; the man who abandons society is the most developed personality in the anonymous caste society. In this respect the *sannyasi* is a revolution behind the man of technopolis, who gains his freedom by benefiting all, and not (like the

[9] A. H. Van den Heuvel, *The Humiliation of the Church* (London, 1966), pp. 78-91.
[10] R. Tagore, *The Religion of Man* (London & New York, 1912), p. 96.
[11] H. Cox, *The Secular City* (London, 1968), pp. 51-71.

man who abandons society) at their expense. The one buys his freedom at the cost of his renunciation of society, the other at the cost of his commitment; the hippy would like it for nothing.

Modern society gives everyone the freedom which Hindu society only gives to the small élite of its *sannyasi*; the young Indians who rebel against these restrictions are asking the West to free them from them. This liberation produces man in a state of solitude, and this is its real problem. To break this solitude by going backwards (the Jesus movement) or by a flight to something foreign (the Hare Krishna cult) is a desperate attempt on the part of some young people. Is the *regressio ad originem* advocated by the very people who are helping us to analyse our distress any less desperate?[12] It looks too much like a *post factum* justification to be any real use in helping the first generation in technopolis to live with its solitude.

Without claiming to have discovered a more satisfactory "way" than that proposed by Harvey Cox or Erich Fromm, I do think that the study of comparative religion can make a contribution to the common investigation.

My familiarity with *Brahman* makes it impossible for me to adopt the myth of the "return to the origins". Hinduism has made the legitimate pluralism in religious experience into a hierarchical system. I should never have spoken, as I have throughout this article, of one Hindu God; there are in fact as many Hindu gods as there are types of religious experience. The God of the *sannyasi* is certainly the highest, but there is also the God of the *bhakta*, the God of the *karmayogi*, the God of the follower of *dharma*, and the God of the untouchable. At each of these "levels" the existential relation between man and God is different, and is expressed in specific rituals. There are no pilgrimages to the God of the *sannyasi*, but the salvation will not be expected from him that the *bhakta* awaits from his *avatar*. Hinduism must teach Christianity to look at itself with more objectivity. The Yahweh of the final editor of Genesis is not, in the eyes of the religious historian, the Yahweh of Erich Fromm, nor is the God of Isaac the God of Jesus or Harvey Cox. On the other hand, the God of the crusades and the God of Sala-ud-din were

---

[12] E. Fromm, *You shall be as Gods* (Greenwich, 1966), p. 14; H. Cox, *The Secular City Debate* (London & New York, 1966), p. 182.

the same. Obviously, I am not talking here of the God of faith, but of God as he comes into existential relation with man, and determines man's attitude and ritual.

The man of technopolis is being forced to live in an existential relation to God which cannot be reduced to any of the types of experience already integrated into the traditional religions. One element in this new relation is a freedom from the tyranny of the group with regard to the choice of possible experiences; another may well be the new type of relation to others and to physical nature imposed on its members by the society of technopolis.

On the horizontal plane the young are "rediscovering" *bhakti*: mysticism and communal celebration. This is a necessary "return to the origins" which enables Westerners to recover types of religious experience which recent Christianity has undervalued. The only really new element in this is the non-sectarianism of a search which wants to claim the inheritance of the whole of man's religious history.[13]

On the vertical plane, we are emerging into a new continent. Socialization and psychoanalysis and all its developments (group dynamics, etc.) seem bound to produce a more radically trinitarian religious experience than anything the religions of the world have known so far. This brings us back to the profound intuition of Monchanin that India would give the Church its theology of the Trinity.

It is not the Hindu God in his hippy *avatar* who will cure us of our despair, but rather the return shock of the dialogue opened by the "third man" of our society with the Hindu God challenged by the Indian "third man". The exciting adventure of the man of the third cycle is only just beginning.[14]

*Translated by Francis McDonagh*

---

[13] G. Moran, *The New Community* (New York, 1970), pp. 29 ff.

[14] B. J. Cooke, *Theology in an Age of Revolution* (Denville, N.J., n.d.), pp. 124–43. The third cycle is a modification of the typology proposed by Harvey Cox (tribal-urban-technopolitan) as follows: the cycle of cosmobiological religions; the cycle of historical religions (the age of the great religions); the cycle of humanist religions. Within each cycle types of structures recurring in each religion could be distinguished. For the second cycle, for example, there would be soteriological, mystical, sacramental, legalistic structures, and so on.

# PART III
## STATEMENT

# Prefatory Note to
# Erich Fromm's Article

The following contribution appears in place of the usual docu-
mentation. For want of a universally satisfactory heading, we
have decided to call the section STATEMENT(S). Whenever it
seems apt (and possible), non-Christian authors of international
status will write here on the theme of the particular issue. This
would seem especially important in the case of fundamental
theology and at critical junctures. In this way we hope to be able
to subject our complex of themes to the effective tendencies and
intellectual contexts in the world today, before which Christians
are answerable for their hope. Our confidence that theology can
also learn a lot and find out something about itself in the process
does not seem unfounded.

The authors who write for this section are asked not so much
for an article from their "specialism" as for a general though
individually nuanced point of view. It is in this sense that the
following statement by Erich Fromm is to be understood.

J. B. METZ

Erich Fromm

# Some Post-Marxian and
# Post-Freudian Thoughts on
# Religion and Religiousness

Marx and Freud are usually treated as materialistic atheists and enemies of religion. In a very general sense, this is true (though of course one has to distinguish between Freud's bourgeois materialism and Marx's historical materialism); on closer inspection, however, this categorization is in many respects questionable.

True, Marx was an opponent of religion. But ultimately his critique was a protest against religion as providing only an illusory satisfaction of man's spiritual needs.

What were these needs as far as Marx was concerned: as he saw them from the *Philosophic Manuscripts* to the last volume of *Capital*?

An end to the stunting and alienation of man; a love that would allow him to believe in the reality of the objective world outside him; riches from the wealth of genuine human needs. Man has to become "poor", for this poverty leads to the experience of the greatest riches: the other man. "The less you *are* and the less you afford expression to this life, the more you have and the greater your alienated life. . . ." The criticism of economics and politics is the prerequisite for the humanization of man—for his return to himself. For Marx, the man of history to date is not what he *ought to be*; but he ought to be what he *can be*, if he frees himself from his enslavement to things and thus from his self-enslavement.

Man's harmony with nature, with his fellow men and with himself is the ultimate goal of Marx's socialism. Marx believed that only an altered practical life (*praxis*) would enable man to learn the truth about himself and the goal of human development—an idea that, in principle, he had in common with religion, in so far as religious *practice* is the prerequisite for religious knowledge. The difference is that, for Marx, man has to change the practice of life as a whole (that is, the socio-economic structure), if he is to realize himself as a loving, knowing and free being.

Marx is an "atheistic-religious" thinker; anyone who reads him without the falsifying spectacles of reformist and Soviet "socialism" can hardly deny the inward connection with the Buddhist (and Zen-Buddhist) position, or with Christian mysticism, and especially that most radical of mystics, Meister Eckhart. Perhaps one might even say that Marx is the most consistent representative of "negative theology". He talks not about God but about idols and alienated—that is, idolatrous—man. Of course, as Löwith and others have shown, in essence the Marxian vision of socialism expresses in secular language the ideas of the prophets of the "messianic age".

*Freud*'s relation to religion is different in kind. Freud was a rationalist: a bourgeois, and not an historical, materialist. His critique of religion was directed from other angles. Religion, said Freud, stultifies man because it allows him to believe in myths instead of in scientifically grounded facts. It infantilizes him, because it keeps him permanently dependent on paternal authority, symbolized by the God image.

In this respect, Freud by and large repeats the traditional atheistic criticism of religion, and has just as little comprehension as that convention of subjective religious *experience*, especially the mystical variety, which is least open to anti-authoritarian criticism. For Freud, the experience of mystical union (which Romain Rolland once called "oceanic emotion") was nothing but a "regression" to primary infantile narcissism.

Freud's objectives for human life were essentially those of the rationalistic thinker: control of his own nature and domination of the feeling of powerlessness in regard to nature without. *"Sapere aude"*, the motto of the Enlightenment, was his motto, too; just as much as the goal of independence—though contrary to Marx—in the sense of bourgeois individualism. His creative

achievement was to go beyond the rationalism of the Enlightenment and establish a "science of the irrational". Freud was a
sceptical and resigned man (especially in the period after the
First World War); he was the last great man of the Enlightenment, but in contrast to Marx he was not at all religious, just as
he was not literary. He was almost wholly without any association with art and literature. It is certainly just to say that he
wanted to solve all human problems exclusively with thought,
and that many of his interpretations have something obsessional
about them.

But, in several respects, Freud's work can still help to illuminate
the religious problem. First of all he revealed the opposition between conscious *thought* and the *unconscious experiences* behind
it, and in this way extended the concept of integrity. Until Freud,
anyone who believed what he said was honest. Freud showed that
only those are honest whose thinking corresponds to their unconscious affects and longings. Freud, the rationalist, admittedly did
not deny, but—paradoxically—relativized the meaning of ideas
and mental concepts. Somewhat roughly summarized: what a
man *thinks* is not so important; what he—consciously or unconsciously—*experiences*, or more simply—what he *is*, is much more
significant. The thesis that the intellect is the best that we possess,
and yet is so weak in contrast to the feelings, is one of the basic
principles of Freud's thought, which leads to an ambivalent esti-
mate of thinking.

With this critique of consciousness, Freud (so it seems to me),
even though very indirectly, contributed to the understanding of
negative theology in the philosophy of religion, and to the God
concept. If thought concepts are important only against the background of the reality of the experiences upon which they are
grounded, then theological concepts are of only secondary importance in comparison with religious experience. Despite the great
difference between negative theology and mysticism, there is a
common factor: a refusal to conceive God in the categories of
thought. In fact, the Neo-Platonists, Dionysius, Maimonides,
Meister Eckhart and the author of the *Cloud of Unknowing*
share the idea that knowledge of God lies in the knowledge of
his unknowability. For the radical mystics there is only one way

to God—that of "naked intent" and a consciousness free of *thought*.

Freud's importance for the problem of "religiousness" has another aspect. Two central religious categories, that of *self-knowledge* and that of *humility* (or of *pride*), can be valuably enriched by Freud's work.

First of all, a word about self-knowledge. Aquinas teaches that humility is self-knowledge, which sees the unworthiness of man even though it does not ignore his worth. Similarly, the author of the *Cloud of Unknowing*, even more drastically than Aquinas, sees self-knowledge as the knowledge of human wickedness; both, in this respect, are very close to Freud's theory. In Eckhart we find a much more far-reaching concept of self-knowledge. Not only in the sense of the conditions appertaining to the knowledge of God ("For no one can know God, who has not first of all known himself"), but mainly in the fact that for Eckhart self-knowledge means knowledge of the whole man and not primarily his unworthiness. Self-knowledge is at the same time knowledge of the other, "as though all human nature were contained in thee and thy nature in anybody's nature, thou seeing thyself in everyone and everyone in thee"). The role of self-knowledge in Buddhism is very beautifully described in Nyaponika Thera's book on Buddhist meditation.

For Freud, self-knowledge is the central category of his entire work and the basic principle of his therapy. But we have to ask whether religious thinkers mean the same thing as Freud when they talk of "self-knowledge"?

Of course there are major differences. Freud's "self" is the *ego*, a substance, something that I *have*, that he wants to intensify and not (as, for instance, Eckhart) lose. Of course Freud expected to see in the unconscious essentially only the impulsive and irrational, and especially the sexual, and not the more profound dimensions of experience, which have their source in the *conditio humana*.

Despite the restrictions of Freud's concept of "self-knowledge", his achievement was to allow access to the unconscious, and thus immeasurably to enrich the possibility of self-knowledge, and to develop a *method* of advancing self-knowledge by dream-interpretation, "Freudian slips", day-dreams, fantasies, free associations, and much more besides.

Freud did not think that his method could have any application beyond the therapeutic; or perhaps, to put it better, any that could serve the mental therapy of the "normal", "healthy" man, who is sick in his soul, because he has been adapted to a sick society. He did not go beyond the sociologico-biological concept of health in the sense of proficient functioning, and attain to the position of those religious thinkers (or that of Marx—"non-stultified" man) who see man's cure in the unfolding of his love, his live, critical reason, and his humility.

Freud did not think about such a cure, but his *method* of analysis can be very significant for man's spiritual development, if he uses it to see himself just as he is, quite naked, and not in the clothing and mask (*persona*) supplied by society. To see oneself as one is does not mean only to see one's vices and weaknesses, but *oneself*, the whole man as one was when one was born, as one is today, and as one will be, or could be. Psychoanalysis as a period of training for this method, and daily self-analysis, can in fact become a major spiritual practice.

Another important religious concept, that of *humility*, can be more proficiently understood by means of psychoanalysis. For modern man, at least, humility is something worn-out and imprecise. Is humility the same as modesty, self-denial? Has humility something to do with the mystical notion of "self-emptying", "being-dead", or the Buddhist notion of "non-desire"?

The concept of humility is perhaps best comprehended by means of its opposite, *pride*; no further words are needed to explain the central role of pride as the primal sin in the Christian view of things.

Certainly, theological formulations such as *ego sum, ego sum et nemo* (Augustine), or the definition of pride as "ego-centredness and you-lessness" and certain other descriptions, are very clear. I think that the Freudian concept of *narcissism* adds a certain clarification—both as a definition of pride and of humility in the sense of non-narcissism.

"Primary narcissism" was for Freud the phenomenon that all the infant's libido affected only the infant and not, as yet, objects outside the infant's self; he supposed that in the process of maturation, libido turned itself outwards, but that in sick states it again dissociated itself from objects and was directed back upon oneself ("secondary narcissism"). Freud's concept of narcissism was quite restricted, for it relied on libido theory and because it was applied mainly to the problems of the mentally sick. The narcissism of the "normal" individual, on the other hand, received little attention. In order to understand this "normal" narcissism, we would do better to separate it from the Freudian concept of libido and to describe it as follows. For the narcissistic individual, only that is real and important which has to do with himself: with *his* body, *his* wishes, *his* thoughts; everything "outside" is apprehended sensuously and conceptually, but it remains grey and nothing but an *object of thought*. The narcissist cannot love; yet one cannot say that he loves himself, but that at most he desires himself: he is egotistic, "selfish", "full of himself". For the same reason, he cannot know himself, for he *is* in his own way, because he is so full of himself that neither he himself, nor the world, nor God can become the object of his knowing. Of course, narcissism has its biological foundations: from the standpoint of self-preservation, it would seem to be a rule that one's own life is more important than that of another. This probably explains why narcissism has such strength, and why constant effort is needed to overcome it or effectively to diminish it. This diminution of narcissism is the condition of love *and* of knowledge, and the central norm common to Buddhism, Judaism and Christianity that they have spoken about under various titles. It seems to me that further study of narcissism beyond the principles supplied by Freud is very important for the understanding of the concept and practice of humility.

Marxian and post-Freudian "atheistic religiosity" has received as yet little consideration in the dialogue between Catholics and Marxists. On the one side there are orthodox Christians, on the other men of good will who devote themselves to the cause of peace, justice, solidarity and respect for human dignity. These are goals which derive from Christian belief, and so it is important, given these common goals, to emphasize what is common to Christians and Marxists. We should not forget that many—though not all—Marxists who take part in this discussion are in their attitude to religion closer to the view of it taken by Freud than to that taken by Marx. But I think that dialogue between the radical-Christian and the non-Christian positions is perhaps just as important as that to date. Even though both groups have different concepts, they nevertheless share the same "religious pitch", and a radicalism of attitude. They both start with the assumption that modern industrial society in its capitalist and Soviet forms is irreconcilable with true religiousness; they share the belief that a society, whose goal is consumption, whose moral principle is that of relentless egotism, and whose human result is totally alienated man, is without vitality, and despite its material power must be brought low by reason of its spiritual poverty. They are primarily concerned not with theological concepts, but with the reality of religious experience.

What is the religious situation at the moment? The spirit of capitalism has reduced the religious content of Marxism and of the Church to a minimum. On the other hand, there are millions of men, and especially of young people, who in the midst of "progress" sense the emptiness and deceptiveness of life. They ask: Who am I? Has life got a meaning, and if so, what is it? What can I plan or do in order to escape from the meaninglessness, boredom and despair that result from the fact that I have no centre?

These are genuine questions. They are not invented and do not form part of an ideology. They are spoken out of a profound despair. Most of those who pose these questions now hardly believe that there is any answer to them. Others try to escape despair by reverting to primitive forms of religion; the ritual intoxication, sexual orgy, sadistic perversion, and even "neo-Satanism". Others seek "religion" and "inner liberation". Unfortunately they often fall into the hands of charlatans, whether imported or domestic, who offer for sale the religious ideas of the Orient, often mixed with Freud and "sexual liberation". Young people haven't seen anything better and therefore confuse the genuine with the fake.

It seems to me that the common concern of Christian as of non-Christian religiousness is to speak about the essential part of the "religious tendency", as it can be described in a language understood by those who suffer under their alienation; about the minimum requirements in regard to patience, self-discipline and practice if one is just to take the first steps; and about how one is to distinguish the genuine from the false, truth from deception, and not judge another human directly, according to *what* he says, but according to *how he is.*

Finally, there is another common task which precedes even those already mentioned: the *criticism of idolatry.*

What is an idol in the Old Testament sense? The definition is quite unequivocal: it is a *thing*, a work of human hands to which man submits. The service of idols is the reification and alienation of the living man. God is the nameless and living. Idols are dead things, and those who pray to them become dead things. Idolatry is the self-denial of man as a living being.

The idols of modern, greedy, alienated man are production, consumption, technology, the despoiling of nature. His belief is to expect salvation as the total conquest of nature; he believes that in the end he will himself become God: he replicates the creation—only he is better at it, being a scientist. The richer his idols, the poorer a man is. Instead of joy, the search is for satisfaction and arousal. Instead of being, man looks for having and using. Instead of the living, he chooses the dead. For Marx, *capital* was the expression of the dead and buried; *work*, on the other hand, was the expression of living; hence his voice was prophetic and anti-idolatrous.

Whereas "theology" is not common to radical Christians and non-Christians, they nevertheless share a conviction of what is the essence and the evil of idolatry, whether they use this term, or its synonym, "alienation". From the standpoint of a radical negative theology, it is a problem for Christians whether the theo-logy is possible or permissible.

Whatever the case, "ido-logy"—the science of idols—is possible and necessary. "Idology" is possible because idols are things which one can make and therefore know. It is necessary because the idols do not announce themselves as such. They are no longer called Baal and Astarte, and do not belong to a specific alien "religion"; on the contrary, they bear respectable names, such as "honour" or "state sovereignty"; they are supposed to be wholly rational, like technology; objects of the striving proper to human nature, such as consumption; finally, even God himself becomes an idol in whose name all false deities are blessed.

Radical criticism of society and religion has a religious function: it is the exposure of idols and hence the condition for true religiousness. The disclosure of the idols and struggle against them form the bond that joins or (as I think) should join religious men, Christian and non-theist, together.

*Translated by John Griffiths*

# Biographical Notes

MARC ALYN was born in 1937 in France. A poet and writer, he was awarded the "Max Jacob" Prize for his first collection of poems, *Le Temps des autres*. A critic with *Figaro littéraire*, then with *Figaro*, he has written a number of critical works, notably on François Mauriac, Gérard de Nerval and Dylan Thomas. He has published various collections of poems (*Délébiles*, 1962; *Nuit majeure*, 1968; *Infini au-delà*, 1972), a novel (*Le Déplacement*) and a play (*Le Grand Labyrinthe*, 1971).

GREGORY BAUM, O.S.A., was born 20 June 1923 in Berlin, and ordained in 1954. He studied at the University of Fribourg and at McMaster University, Hamilton (Canada). Master of arts, doctor of theology, he is professor of theology at St Michael's College, University of Toronto. He is also editor of *The Ecumenist* and associate editor of the *Journal of Ecumenical Studies*. Among his published works are: *The Credibility of the Church Today* (1968), *Faith and Doctrine* (1969) and *Man Becoming* (1970).

Guy Deleury, s.j., was born 3 September 1922 in Paris and ordained in 1955. He studied at the Sorbonne, Poona University, the French School of the Far East and the School of Eastern Languages (Paris). Doctor of philosophy, he was co-founder of "Sneha-Sadan" (centre for the dialogue between Hinduism and Catholicism) and formed a youth organization for the Hindu and Moslem communities in Poona. At present he is engaged in writing. Among his published works are: *Le Culte de Vithoba* (Poona, 1960), *Psaumes du Pèlerin* (Paris, 1956) and *La Quête de l'éternel* (Louvain, 1967).

André Dumas was born in 1918 in Montauban and ordained in the Reformed Church in 1950. He studied at Montpellier University and at the Faculties of Protestant Theology of Montpellier, Paris and Basle. Licentiate of philosophy, with a diploma in higher Greek and German studies, he is professor of philosophy and of ethics at the Faculty of Protestant Theology, Paris. Among his published works are: *Le Contrôle des naissances: Opinions protestantes* (Paris, 1964), *Une théologie de la réalité: Dietrich Bonhoeffer* (1967), and *Prospective et prophéties. Les églises dans la société industrielle* (Paris, 1972).

Alain Durand, o.p., was born 26 September 1937 in Virieu-sur-Bourbre (France) and ordained in 1964. He studied at the Dominican Studium of the Arbresle (Lyons) and at Union Theological Seminary (New York). He is editor of *Lumière et Vie* and a member of the Study Centre, "Economie et Humanisme". He is the author of many articles, notably in *Lumière et Vie*, and of *Sécularisation et présence de Dieu* (Paris, 1971).

Erich Fromm was born 23 March 1900 in Frankfurt. He studied at the Universities of Frankfurt, Heidelberg and Munich. Doctor of philosophy, with a diploma in psychoanalysis, he was professor of psychology at Michigan State University from 1955 to 1966 and is now head of the Department of Psychoanalysis in the School of Medicine of the National University of Mexico. Among his published works are: *Psychoanalysis and Religion, The Forgotten Language, The Art of Loving* and *Marx's Concept of Man*.

Claude Geffré, o.p., was born 23 January 1926 in Niort (France) and ordained in 1953. He studied at Saint-Sulpice Seminary, Paris, and at the Dominican Faculties of the Saulchoir. Doctor of theology, he is professor of dogmatic theology at the Saulchoir (since 1957) and professor at the Faculty of Theology of the Institut Catholique, Paris. He has contributed articles to many journals, including *Concilium*.

Jacques Kamstra was born 29 May 1926 in Arnhem and ordained in 1952. From 1954 to 1960 he was a missionary in Japan. Later he studied the history of religions at Nijmegen University. Doctor of theology, he is professor of phenomenology and of living non-Christian religions at the Faculty of Protestant Theology of the University of Amsterdam.

Johannes Baptist Metz was born 5 August 1928 in Welluck (Germany) and ordained in 1954. He studied at the Universities of Innsbruck and Munich. Doctor of philosophy and of theology, he is professor of fundamental theology at the University of Münster. Among his published works are: *Christliche Anthropozentrik* (Munich, 1962), *Zur Theologie der Welt* (1968), *Politische Theologie* ... (1969)—all three of these books have been translated into many languages—*Befreindes Gedächtnis Jesu Christi* (1970) and *Die Theologie in der interdisziplinären Forschung* (1971).

JÜRGEN MOLTMANN was born 8 April 1926 in Hamburg and is a member of the Reformed Evangelical Church. He studied at the University of Göttingen, gaining a doctorate in theology. He was professor at the Ecclesiastical Academy of Wuppertal from 1958 to 1963 and professor of systematic theology at the University of Bonn from 1963 to 1967; he is now professor for the same discipline at the University of Tübingen. He is also editor of *Evangelische Theologie*. Among his published works are: *Prädestination und Perseveranz* (1961), *Theologie der Hoffnung* (1968⁸), *Perspektiven der Theologie* (1968), *Der Mensch* (1971) and *Die ersten Freigelassenen der Schöpfung* (1971²).

KLAUS SCHÄFER was born 3 June 1936 in Stuttgart and ordained in 1968. He studied at the Universities of Tübingen, Bonn, Munich and Copenhagen. Doctor of theology, he is bursar of the Society of Scientific Research of Germany.

NORBERT SCHIFFERS was born 14 June 1926 in Aix-la-Chapelle and ordained in 1952. Doctor of theology after studying at the University of Tübingen, he is professor of fundamental theology at the University of Ratisborn. Among his published works are: *Einheit der Kirche* (Düsseldorf, 1956) and *Fragen der Physik an die Theologie* (Düsseldorf, 1968).

KAREL SKALICKÝ was born 20 May 1934 in Hluboka (Czechoslovakia). He studied at the University of Prague and at the Lateran University. Licentiate of philosophy and doctor of theology, he is professor at the Faculty of Theology of the Lateran University. He is also editor of the review of philosophy and theology *Studie* (Rome). He has published an important commentary on the Pastoral Constitution *Gaudium et Spes* and various articles on revisionist Marxism (Bloch, Gardavský), on theology and on hermeneutics.

## DATE DUE

| DEC 0 8 1995 | | | |
|---|---|---|---|
| APR 2 1 1997 | | | |
| | | | |
| | | | |
| | | | |
| | | | |
| | | | |
| | | | |
| | | | |
| | | | |
| | | | |
| | | | |
| | | | |
| | | | |
| | | | |
| | | | |
| | | | |
| GAYLORD | | | PRINTED IN U.S.A. |